Credits

Author
Ryad El-Dajani

Reviewers
José Manuel Cerrejón González

Kenny Hsu

Michał Piątkowski

Commissioning Editor
Priya Singh

Acquisition Editor
Sam Wood

Content Development Editor
Arwa Manasawala

Technical Editor
Pankaj Kadam

Copy Editor
Laxmi Subramanian

Project Coordinator
Shweta H. Birwatkar

Proofreader
Safis Editing

Indexer
Rekha Nair

Production Coordinator
Manu Joseph

Cover Work
Manu Joseph

About the Author

Ryad El-Dajani is a software engineer and passionate technology enthusiast. He developed an interest in computers when he was 10 years old. Soon thereafter, he began to learn his first programming languages.

After he had completed his training as an IT specialist, he worked on several e-commerce Internet projects. Currently, he is studying business computing and works for a big IT company in Germany, realizing various IT projects based on Java or .NET technologies.

Besides the classic application development, he has professional experience in realizing projects based on web frameworks such as Spring, Play, Symfony, eZ Publish, and Magento. Moreover, he has been excited about all kinds of Unix-like embedded systems since the revolutionary SheevaPlug.

I would like to thank my family for their support during the authoring of this book. Special thanks go to my grandpa, Jürgen, and my uncle, Thomas, who introduced me into the world of computers against the wishes of my parents when I was a child.

Furthermore, I would like to thank the Internet community for spreading their knowledge. Without amazing guys like you, I would have never been able to understand and, in the end, write about the complex technologies surrounding us today.

I am particularly grateful to my beloved girlfriend, Marlene. Without her infinite support, patience, understanding, and cooking skills, I would not have been able to complete this project.

About the Reviewers

José Manuel Cerrejón González is a full-stack freelance software developer based in Huelva, Spain, and a Raspberry Pi, Odroid, and Banana Pi enthusiast. Nowadays, he blogs regularly on his own website at `http://misapuntesde.com/` in both Spanish and English, and he has compiled a great Raspberry Pi resource on Google Docs at `http://goo.gl/Iwhbq`.

He has also contributed to the community with a project called PiKISS (Pi Keeping It Simple, Stupid!) that you can download from GitHub (`https://github.com/jmcerrejon/PiKISS`).

Although this is the first book he has reviewed, he has written other articles for the press, such as ODROID Magazine.

You can follow him on Twitter at `https://twitter.com/ulysess10`.

To my daughter, Laura: I hope to see your smile every morning for a long time.

Kenny Hsu is a Linux system administrator, database administrator, and web developer who has over 7 years of experience. He has executed projects in a broad range of technologies, including Java, Spring Framework, jQuery, MySQL, MariaDB, Ubuntu, Debian, and so on. He is also an open source contributor. This year, he has written some dev board-related tutorials for beginners (who are interested in Banana Pi, Cubieboard, and OpenWRT router), in Chinese. He is also a native Chinese speaker residing in Taiwan.

Some of the tutorials he wrote earlier this year are as follows:

  ▸ OpenWRT wr841n mod (`https://github.com/annbigbig/wr841nd-memo`)

  ▸ Cubian memo (`https://github.com/annbigbig/cubian_memo`)

If you can speak Chinese, you can interact with him directly in Chinese. He would be very glad to talk to you. You can follow him on Twitter at `@annbigbig` and you can also e-mail him at `annbigbig@gmail.com`.

This is my first book with Packt Publishing, and I am very glad to meet you.

My dear kitten called PaPa passed away in summer 2013. He was a 17-year-old white Persian kitten, and I will always miss him.

Michał Piątkowski is a young freelancer, who always tries to develop his potential. Although he mainly programs in Java, he is also interested in C and C++, especially where microcontrollers are concerned. Moreover, he is fascinated by Banana Pi and Raspberry Pi projects. He devotes his spare time to robotics and electronics. On the Internet, he can be found as Axandar or `@Axandar29` on Twitter.

www.PacktPub.com

Support files, eBooks, discount offers, and more

For support files and downloads related to your book, please visit www.PacktPub.com.

Did you know that Packt offers eBook versions of every book published, with PDF and ePub files available? You can upgrade to the eBook version at www.PacktPub.com and as a print book customer, you are entitled to a discount on the eBook copy. Get in touch with us at service@packtpub.com for more details.

At www.PacktPub.com, you can also read a collection of free technical articles, sign up for a range of free newsletters and receive exclusive discounts and offers on Packt books and eBooks.

https://www2.packtpub.com/books/subscription/packtlib

Do you need instant solutions to your IT questions? PacktLib is Packt's online digital book library. Here, you can search, access, and read Packt's entire library of books.

Why Subscribe?

- Fully searchable across every book published by Packt
- Copy and paste, print, and bookmark content
- On demand and accessible via a web browser

Free Access for Packt account holders

If you have an account with Packt at www.PacktPub.com, you can use this to access PacktLib today and view 9 entirely free books. Simply use your login credentials for immediate access.

Table of Contents

Preface   **iii**

Chapter 1: Installation and Setup   **1**

Introduction   1

Downloading an operating system for the Banana Pi   5

Setting up the SD card on Windows   8

Setting up the SD card on Linux   12

Booting up and shutting down the Banana Pi   15

Chapter 2: Administration   **19**

Introduction   19

Determining the IP address and hostname   20

Connecting via SSH on Windows using PuTTY   22

Connecting via SSH on Unix-like systems   27

User maintenance   29

Searching, installing, and removing the software   33

Updating the operating system   37

Wireless network on the Banana Pro   41

Chapter 3: External Disks   **49**

Introduction   49

Mounting a USB drive   49

Mounting an SSD or HDD via SATA   54

Mounting via fstab   56

Booting from an external disk   59

Chapter 4: Networking   **65**

Introduction   65

Sharing files over the network via Samba   65

Setting up a web application   75

Securing the Nginx web server using SSL   87

Synchronizing files over the Internet	92
Controlling the desktop remotely using VNC	104
Securing SSH using SSH keys	109
Setting up a UPnP media server	115
Chapter 5: Using the GPIO Pins	**119**
Introduction	119
Lighting up an LED using the gpio command	120
Programming the LED	127
Using the GPIO input with a pushbutton	134
Chapter 6: Multimedia	**141**
Introduction	141
Configuring the audio device	142
Getting accelerated video playback	147
Setting up Kodi	160
Setting up an infrared remote control using LIRC	166
Index	**175**

Preface

Packed with recipes for the Banana Pi, solving the most common real-world problems, viewers get a practical assistance to avoid difficulties.

Full of supportive guides, this book is designed to help you build and expand your device into a versatile box. Any computer enthusiast can quickly learn how to become a Banana Pi expert, while not requiring skills in programming or Linux. *Banana Pi Cookbook* will allow you to use the technology start from the very beginning, through the daily usage and maintenance, up to setting up a WordPress from scratch, sharing files using Samba or ownCloud, blinking an LED, or playing 1080p videos.

What this book covers

Chapter 1, *Installation and Setup*, introduces the Banana Pi device. It also explains which distributions are available and how to download and install a Linux distribution. Moreover, we present Android as a contrast to our upcoming Linux adventure.

Chapter 2, *Administration*, introduces the reader to the most common tools to administrate their fresh Linux installation. We will connect remotely using SSH from Windows (using PuTTY) and Linux (using the command-line SSH application). Besides user modification (adding a new user, changing passwords, and so on), we will also cover basic maintenance tasks, such as searching and installing a new software, updating the system using the distributions package manager, and so on.

Chapter 3, *External Disks*, covers all about external disk drives. We will connect and mount USB drives and HDD drives using the SATA interface and explore the possibility of switching the root filesystem to and boot from an external drive.

Chapter 4, *Networking*, presents recipes for common networking tasks using the Banana Pi. One of the key strengths of the device is the fast Ethernet and wireless (Banana Pro) adapters it provides—especially combined with the fast SATA interface—which is the base of powerful network applications.

Chapter 5, Using the GPIO Pins, introduces the GPIO pins. We will light up an LED using the shell. Furthermore, we will build a simple circuit, including a pull-up resistor and control an LED with a button. To achieve this, we will introduce the C programming language with the WiringPi library and the Python scripting language with the RPi.GPIO library.

Chapter 6, Multimedia, covers configuring the two audio outputs (line out and HDMI). We will discuss and solve the hardware acceleration problem by compiling important components and using these mentioned components to build video players and Kodi. The configuration of a remote control using LIRC is also covered.

What you need for this book

The following is a list of things that you'll need to follow along with the recipes of this book:

- ► A Banana Pi and/or a Banana Pro
- ► An SD card
- ► An SD card reader
- ► A 5V USB power supply
- ► A network connection (Ethernet and/or WiFi on Banana Pro)
- ► An HDMI or a composite connection for display
- ► A USB keyboard and a mouse
- ► A Windows or Linux operating system
- ► An external HDD/SSD plus a power supply and a SATA connection for *Chapter 3, External Disks*
- ► A breadboard and various electrical components for *Chapter 5, Using the GPIO Pins*

Who this book is for

This book is intended for anybody who wants to learn how they can utilize the capabilities of the Banana Pi to its full potential. It's full of step-by-step guides and detailed descriptions for the whole range of possibilities in a language that is appropriate for computer enthusiasts and experts alike. It would be helpful to have a basic knowledge of Unix-like operating systems or programming, but no prior experience is required as every concept is explained in the appropriate sections.

Sections

In this book, you will find several headings that appear frequently (Getting ready, How to do it, How it works, There's more, and See also).

To give clear instructions on how to complete a recipe, we use these sections as follows:

Getting ready

This section tells you what to expect in the recipe, and describes how to set up any software or any preliminary settings required for the recipe.

How to do it...

This section contains the steps required to follow the recipe.

How it works...

This section usually consists of a detailed explanation of what happened in the previous section.

There's more...

This section consists of additional information about the recipe in order to make the reader more knowledgeable about the recipe.

See also

This section provides helpful links to other useful information for the recipe.

Conventions

In this book, you will find a number of text styles that distinguish between different kinds of information. Here are some examples of these styles and an explanation of their meaning.

Code words in text, database table names, folder names, filenames, file extensions, pathnames, dummy URLs, user input, and Twitter handles are shown as follows: "The commands used in the next steps assume that your SD card is recognized as `/dev/mmcblk0`."

A block of code is set as follows:

```
allow-hotplug wlan0
iface wlan0 inet manual
wpa-roam /etc/wpa_supplicant/wpa_supplicant.conf
```

Any command-line input or output is written as follows:

```
$ sudo cp interfaces interfaces.backup
```

New terms and **important words** are shown in bold. Words that you see on the screen, for example, in menus or dialog boxes, appear in the text like this: "Choose the write mode **Startup** and click on **Format to Normal**."

> Warnings or important notes appear in a box like this.

> Tips and tricks appear like this.

Reader feedback

Feedback from our readers is always welcome. Let us know what you think about this book—what you liked or disliked. Reader feedback is important for us as it helps us develop titles that you will really get the most out of.

To send us general feedback, simply e-mail feedback@packtpub.com, and mention the book's title in the subject of your message.

If there is a topic that you have expertise in and you are interested in either writing or contributing to a book, see our author guide at www.packtpub.com/authors.

Customer support

Now that you are the proud owner of a Packt book, we have a number of things to help you to get the most from your purchase.

Downloading the example code

You can download the example code files from your account at http://www.packtpub.com for all the Packt Publishing books you have purchased. If you purchased this book elsewhere, you can visit http://www.packtpub.com/support and register to have the files e-mailed directly to you.

Downloading the color images of this book

We also provide you with a PDF file that has color images of the screenshots/diagrams used in this book. The color images will help you better understand the changes in the output. You can download this file from https://www.packtpub.com/sites/default/files/downloads/2443OS_ColorImages.pdf.

Errata

Although we have taken every care to ensure the accuracy of our content, mistakes do happen. If you find a mistake in one of our books—maybe a mistake in the text or the code—we would be grateful if you could report this to us. By doing so, you can save other readers from frustration and help us improve subsequent versions of this book. If you find any errata, please report them by visiting http://www.packtpub.com/submit-errata, selecting your book, clicking on the **Errata Submission Form** link, and entering the details of your errata. Once your errata are verified, your submission will be accepted and the errata will be uploaded to our website or added to any list of existing errata under the Errata section of that title.

To view the previously submitted errata, go to https://www.packtpub.com/books/content/support and enter the name of the book in the search field. The required information will appear under the **Errata** section.

Piracy

Piracy of copyrighted material on the Internet is an ongoing problem across all media. At Packt, we take the protection of our copyright and licenses very seriously. If you come across any illegal copies of our works in any form on the Internet, please provide us with the location address or website name immediately so that we can pursue a remedy.

Please contact us at copyright@packtpub.com with a link to the suspected pirated material.

We appreciate your help in protecting our authors and our ability to bring you valuable content.

eBooks, discount offers, and more

Did you know that Packt offers eBook versions of every book published, with PDF and ePub files available? You can upgrade to the eBook version at www.PacktPub.com and as a print book customer, you are entitled to a discount on the eBook copy. Get in touch with us at customercare@packtpub.com for more details.

At www.PacktPub.com, you can also read a collection of free technical articles, sign up for a range of free newsletters, and receive exclusive discounts and offers on Packt books and eBooks.

Questions

If you have a problem with any aspect of this book, you can contact us at questions@packtpub.com, and we will do our best to address the problem.

1
Installation and Setup

This chapter will cover the following recipes:

- ▸ Downloading an operating system for the Banana Pi
- ▸ Setting up the SD card on Windows
- ▸ Setting up the SD card on Linux
- ▸ Booting up and shutting down the Banana Pi

Introduction

The Banana Pi is a single-board computer, which enables you to build your own individual and versatile system. In fact, it is a complete computer, including all the required elements such as a processor, memory, network, and other interfaces, which we are going to explore. It provides enough power to run even relatively complex applications suitably.

In this chapter, we are going to get to know the Banana Pi device. The available distributions are mentioned, as well as how to download and install these distributions. We will also examine Android in contrast to our upcoming Linux adventure.

Thus, you are going to transform your little piece of hardware into a functional, running computer with a working operating system. You will master the whole process of doing the required task from connecting the cables, choosing an operating system, writing the image to an SD card, and successfully booting up and shutting down your device for the first time.

Banana Pi Overview

In the following picture, you see a Banana Pi on the left-hand side and a Banana Pro on the right-hand side:

As you can see, there are some small differences that we need to notice. The Banana Pi provides a dedicated composite video output besides the HDMI output. However, with the Banana Pro, you can connect your display via composite video output using a four-pole composite audio/video cable on the jack.

In contrast to the Banana Pi, which has 26 pin headers, the Banana Pro provides 40 pins. Also the pins for the UART port interface are located below the GPIO headers on the Pi, while they are located besides the network interface on the Pro.

The other two important differences are not clearly visible on the previous picture. The operating system for your device comes in the form of image files that need to be written (*burned*) to an SD card. The Banana Pi uses normal SD cards while the Banana Pro will only accept Micro SD cards. Moreover, the Banana Pro provides a Wi-Fi interface already on board. Therefore, you are also able to connect the Banana Pro to your wireless network, while the Pi would require an external wireless USB device.

Besides the mentioned differences, the devices are very similar. You will find the following hardware components and interfaces on your device.

On the back side, you will find:

- A20 ARM Cortex-A7 dual core central processing unit (CPU)
- ARM Mali400 MP2 graphics processing unit (GPU)
- 1 gigabyte of DDR3 memory (that is shared with the GPU)

On the front side, you will find:

- Ethernet network interface adapter
- Two USB 2.0 ports
- A 5V micro USB power with DC in and a micro USB OTG port
- A SATA 2.0 port and SATA power output
- Various display outputs [HDMI, LVDS, and composite (integrated into jack on the Pro)]
- A CSI camera input connector
- An infrared (IR) receiver
- A microphone
- Various hardware buttons on board (power key, reset key, and UBoot key)
- Various LEDs (red for power status, blue for Ethernet status, and green for user defined)

As you can see, you have a lot of opportunities for letting your device interact with various external components. In the upcoming chapters, we are going to explore most of the possibilities in detail.

Operating systems for the Banana Pi

The Banana Pi is capable of running any operating system that supports the ARM Cortex-A7 architecture. There are several operating systems precompiled, so you are able to write the operating system to an SD card and boot your system flawlessly. Currently, there are the following operating systems provided officially by **LeMaker**, the manufacturer of the Banana Pi.

Android

Android is a well-known operating system for mobile phones, but it is also runnable on various other devices such as smart watches, cars, and, of course, single-board computers such as the Banana Pi.

The main advantage of running Android on a single-board computer is its convenience. Anybody who uses an Android-based smartphone will recognize the **graphical user interface** (**GUI**) and may have less initial hurdles. Also, setting up a media center might be easier to do on Android than on a Linux-based system.

However, there are also a few disadvantages, as you are limited to software that is provided by an Android store such as Google Play. As most apps are optimized for mobile use at the moment, you will not find a lot of usable software for your Banana Pi running Android, except some Games and Multimedia applications. Moreover, you are required to use special Windows software called PhoenixCard to be able to prepare an Android SD card.

Because of the mentioned disadvantages, this book will show you how to get Android up and running, but focus on Linux-based distributions in the next chapters.

Linux

Most of the Linux users never realize that they are actually using Linux when operating their phones, appliances, routers, and many more products, as most of its magic happens in the background. We are going to dig into this adventure to discover its possibilities when running on our Banana Pi device.

The following Linux-based operating systems—so-called *distributions*—are used by the majority of the Banana Pi user base and are supported officially by the manufacturer:

- ▶ **Lubuntu**: This is a lightweight distribution based on the well-known Ubuntu using the LXDE desktop, which is principally a good choice, if you are a Windows user.
- ▶ **Raspbian**: This is a distribution based on Debian, which was initially produced for the Raspberry Pi (hence the name). As a lot of Raspberry Pi owners are running Raspbian on their devices while also experimenting with the Banana Pi, LeMaker ported the original Raspbian distribution to the Banana Pi. Raspbian also comes with an LXDE desktop by default.
- ▶ **Bananian**: This too is a Debian-based Linux distribution optimized exclusively for the Banana Pi and its siblings.

All of the aforementioned distributions are based on the well-known distribution, Debian. Besides the huge user base, all Debian-based distributions use the same package manager **Apt** (**Advanced Packaging Tool**) to search for and install new software, and all are similar to use. In the upcoming recipes, we are going to use Raspbian. However, most recipes will be valid for the other Debian-based distributions.

There are still more distributions that are officially supported by LeMaker, such as Berryboot, LeMedia, OpenSUSE, Fedora, Gentoo, Scratch, ArchLinux, Open MediaVault, and OpenWrt. All of them have their pros and cons or their specific use cases. If you are an experienced Linux user, you may choose your preferred distribution from the mentioned list, as most of the recipes in this book are similar to, or even equally usable on, most of the Linux-based operating systems.

Moreover, the Banana Pi community publishes various customized Linux distributions for the Banana Pi regularly. The possible advantages of a customized distribution may include enabled and optimized hardware acceleration capabilities, supportive helper scripts, fully equipped desktop environments, and much more. However, when deciding to use a customized distribution, there is no official support by LeMaker and you have to contact the publisher in case you encounter bugs, or need help.

Downloading an operating system for the Banana Pi

The following two recipes will explain how to set up the SD card with the desired operating system and how to get the Banana Pi up and running for the first time. This recipe is a predecessor, as the required hardware components and the downloaded image is valid for both Windows and Linux systems.

Usually, the Banana Pi is shipped without any other components. Besides the device itself, you will need at least a source for energy, which is usually a USB power supply and an SD card to boot your Banana Pi. Also, a network cable and connection is highly recommended to be able to interact with your Banana Pi from another computer via a *remote shell* using the application SSH (that is covered in the next chapter).

You might also want to actually see something on a display. Then, you will need to connect your Banana Pi via HDMI, composite, or LVDS to an external screen. It is recommended that you use an HDMI Version 1.4 cable since lower versions can possibly cause issues.

Besides inputting data using a remote shell, you can directly connect an USB keyboard and mouse to your Banana Pi via the USB ports.

After completing the required tasks in the upcoming recipes, you will be able to boot your Banana Pi.

The following picture shows a USB power supply, a Banana Pro, and a Micro SD card.

Getting ready

The following components are required for this recipe:

- Banana Pi
- SD card (minimum class 4; class 10 is recommended)
- USB power supply (5V 2A recommended)
- A computer with an SD card reader/writer (to write the image to the SD card)

Furthermore, you are going to need an Internet connection to download a Linux distribution or Android.

A few optional but highly recommended components are:

- Connection to a display (via HDMI or composite)
- Network connection via Ethernet
- USB keyboard and mouse

You can acquire these items from various retailers. All items shown in the previous two pictures were bought from an online retailer that is known for originally selling books. However, the Banana Pi and the other products can be acquired from a large number of retailers. It is recommended to get a USB power supply with 2000mA (2A) output.

How to do it...

To download an operating system for Banana Pi, follow these steps:

1. Download an image of your desired operating system. We are going to download Android and Raspbian from the official LeMaker image files website: `http://www.lemaker.org/resources/9-38/image_files.html`.

    The following screenshot shows the LeMaker website where you can download the official images:

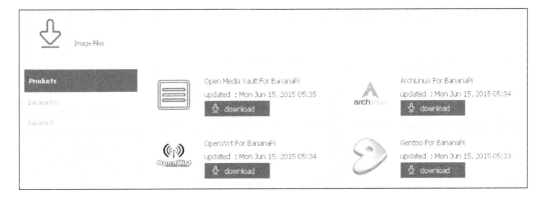

2. If you are clicking on one of the mirrors (such as **Google Drive**, **Dropbox**, and so on), you will be redirected to the equivalent file-hosting service. From there, you are actually able to download the archive file.

3. Once your archive containing the image is downloaded, you are ready to unpack the downloaded archive, which we will do in the upcoming recipes.

See also

▸ LeMaker image files. This is the official location for operating systems by the manufacturer of the Banana Pi—`http://www.lemaker.org/portal.php?mod=list&catid=4`

▸ The *Banana Pi / Arch Linux / Customized Distribution* article on Ryad's blog. This is a customized Arch Linux distribution provided by the author, including a lot of features such as the LXDE desktop environment and enabled hardware acceleration—`http://blog.eldajani.net/banana-pi-arch-linux-customized-distribution/`

Setting up the SD card on Windows

This recipe will explain how to set up the SD card using a Windows operating system.

Getting ready

To prepare your image and the SD card on Windows, you will usually need the following software ingredients:

- A downloaded image from the previous recipe
- 7-Zip
- SD Formatter
- Win32 Disk Imager to write Linux-based operating systems
- PhoenixCard to write the Android operating system

 The upcoming screenshots are showing image files for the Banana Pro. If you are using the Banana Pi, make sure to download and burn the image files for the Banana Pi.

How to do it...

In the upcoming steps, we will unpack the archive containing the operating system image for the Banana Pi and write the image to the SD card:

1. Open the downloaded archive with 7-Zip. The following screenshot shows the 7-Zip application opening a compressed `.tgz` archive:

2. Unpack the archive to a directory until you get a file with the file extension `.img`. If it is `.tgz` or `.tar.gz` file, you will need to unpack the archive twice. The following screenshot shows the final image file with the file extension `.img` and the unpacked and compressed `.tgz` archive:

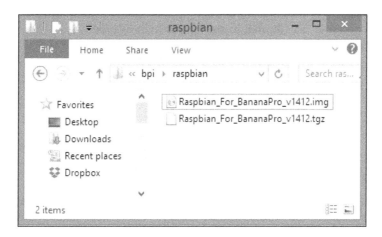

3. Create a backup of the contents of the SD card as everything on the SD card is going to be erased unrecoverablely.

4. Open SD Formatter and check the disk letter (**E:** in the following screenshot).

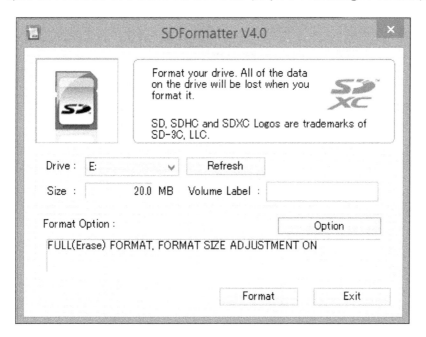

5. Choose **Option** to open the **Option Setting** window and choose:

   - **FORMAT TYPE: FULL (Erase)**
   - **FORMAT SIZE ADJUSTMENT: ON**

6. When everything is configured correctly, check again to see whether you are using the correct disk and click **Format** to start the formatting process.

Writing an Android image to the SD card on Windows

In the following steps, we are writing an Android image to the SD card using Windows:

1. Execute `PhoenixCard.exe`.

2. Choose the Android image file by clicking on **Img File**.

3. Choose the write mode **Startup** and click on **Format to Normal**.

4. You will see a message, that the formatting was successful.

5. After the formatting, click on **Burn** while leaving the write mode as **Startup**. After a few minutes, your SD card should be ready to boot up Android on the Banana Pi.

   The following screenshot shows the PhoenixCard application where the image has been successfully written:

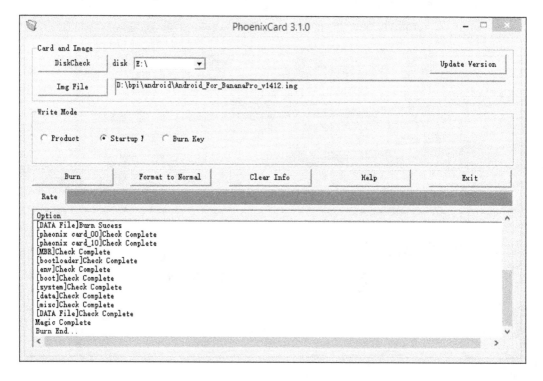

Now you can insert the SD card into your Banana Pi and power it up. After the booting process, you will see the Android operating system.

Writing a Linux distribution image to the SD card on Windows

The following steps explain how to write a Linux-based distribution to the SD card on Windows:

1. Format the SD card using SD Formatter, which we covered in the previous section.

2. Open the Win32 Disk Imager.

3. Choose the image file by clicking on the directory button.

4. Check, whether you are going to write to the correct disk and then click on **Write**. The next screenshot shows the writing operation of Win32 Disk Imager:

Once the burning process is done, you are ready to insert the freshly prepared SD card containing your Linux operating system into the Banana Pi and boot it up for the first time.

How it works...

Some images are archived using Linux archive formats, which Windows may be unable to unpack natively. Therefore, it might be necessary to install a tool which is capable of unpacking the archive. In this recipe, we use 7-Zip to unpack the archives, which is open source software and is easy to use. Some images are also available as ZIP files, which can also be unpacked using 7-Zip or Windows Explorer. To extract the image from a ZIP file using the Windows Explorer, right-click on the ZIP file and select **Extract all**.

Linux archives usually have to be unpacked twice. Firstly, to uncompress the archive (`.tar.gz` or `.tgz`) and secondly, to unpack the actual tar archive (which is used to collect files into one uncompressed file). On Linux, you will be able to unpack the packed archives, and uncompress the compressed archives with one command.

After unpacking the image file and formatting your SD card, you need software to burn the image to the SD card. For Android, you will need the software PhoenixCard, for any other image based on Linux, the software Win32 Disk Imager is required.

See also

  ▶ SD Formatter is free downloadable software by the SD Association to reformat SD cards efficiently and safely. You can get it for the Windows platform at `https://www.sdcard.org/downloads/formatter_4/`

  ▶ PhoenixCard is a specialized tool used to write Android images to the SD card. You can get it for the Windows platform at `https://drive.google.com/file/d/0B_VynIqhAcB7NTg2UkRDdHRWX2s/edit?usp=sharing` or alternatively at `http://download.eldajani.net/bananapi/phoenixcard.zip`

  ▶ Win32 Disk Imager is an open source tool we use to write the operating system images to SD cards. You can get it for the Windows platform at `http://sourceforge.net/projects/win32diskimager/`

Setting up the SD card on Linux

This recipe will explain how to set up the SD card using a Linux-based operating system. On Linux computers, you usually will not need any special software to uncompress archives or write the image to an SD card. To do these tasks, you usually need the command-line tools *tar* and *dd* that are preinstalled on almost any Linux distribution by default.

Getting ready

To prepare your image and the SD card on Linux, you will only need the following software ingredients:

  ▶ A downloaded image from the *Downloading an operating system for the Banana Pi* recipe

  ▶ The dd program

  ▶ The tar program including gzip support

  ▶ Optionally, the fdisk program

How to do it...

The following steps are required to unpack the image archive and write the image to the SD card:

 Use the following dd command **very carefully**. The dd command will overwrite anything on the output (the of parameter). In fact, you can damage your computer, if you choose the wrong output. So, make sure that the value of the parameter of is definitely the SD card.

1. Unpack the downloaded .tar.gz or .tgz archive using the following command:

    ```
    $ tar -xzvf Raspbian_For_BananaPi_v1412.tgz
    ```

2. If you have downloaded a .zip file, you use the following command:

    ```
    $ unzip Raspbian_For_BananaPi_v1412.zip
    ```

3. Determine how your SD card is recognized by the system. You can check the correct path of your SD card by using the following command:

    ```
    $ sudo fdisk -l
    ```

 To determine the correct device, you can compare the results before and after you plug in the SD card.

The commands used in the next steps assume that your SD card is recognized as /dev/mmcblk0.

4. Make a backup of the contents on your SD card.

5. Unmount all partitions of the SD card, if any partition is mounted:

    ```
    $ sudo umount /dev/mmcblk0*
    ```

6. Write the image to the SD card:

    ```
    $ sudo dd if=Raspbian_For_BananaPi_v1412.img of=/dev/mmcblk0 bs=1M
    ```

    The writing process takes a few minutes.

7. On some systems, the SD card is automatically mounted after the writing process. Unmount the partitions of the SD card again:

    ```
    $ sudo umount /dev/mmcblk0*
    ```

When the writing process is finished, you can eject your SD card and put it into the SD slot of your Banana Pi.

How it works...

On Linux, you also need to unpack an image file and write the image to the SD card. Luckily, these tasks are much quicker and more easily done on the command line and you usually do not need to install additional software.

In fact, to unpack the image, you need the `tar` command and to write an image to the SD card you need the `dd` (disk dump) command. The tool tar is a program to pack or unpack archive files. The tool dd is a utility to convert and copy files from a source (the input file—the `if` parameter) to a destination (the output file—the `of` parameter). In contrast to a normal file copy, the actual order of the bytes is preserved.

The `dd` command is executed with root privileges (by using the prefix command `sudo`) to use the image file as input, the SD card as output, and to read/write with a block size (the `bs` parameter) of one megabyte. That block size value is a safe choice when writing images to or reading from SD cards. You can also try a block size value of `4M`, which results in a faster but possibly unsuccessful writing process.

You do not need to format the SD card before issuing the `dd` command as `dd` also writes the whole partition information directly to the SD card.

The output parameter has to be the whole SD card (`/dev/mmcblk0` in our previous example). Make sure not to accidentally write to a partition of the SD card. This means do not use `/dev/mmcblk0p1` or the like).

Moreover, depending on your computer, the SD card may be recognized as `/dev/sdX` and not `/dev/mmcblk0`. Use the `fdisk -l` command to determine the correct device file as mentioned in this recipe.

The `dd` command will take some time. If you want to check the progress, you can issue the following command in another shell:

```
$ sudo pkill -USR1 -n -x dd
```

This will output the current status on the running dd job.

See also

▶ Type in the `man dd` command into a shell to show the manual page of dd:

```
$ man dd
```

▶ Type in the `man tar` command into a shell to show the manual page of tar:

```
$ man tar
```

▶ Type in the `man fdisk` command into a shell to show the manual page of fdisk:

```
$ man fdisk
```

Booting up and shutting down the Banana Pi

This recipe will explain how to boot up and shut down the Banana Pi. As the Banana Pi is a real computer, these tasks are as equally important as tasks on your desktop computer. The booting process starts the Linux kernel and several important services. The shutting down stops them accordingly and does not power off the Banana Pi until all data is synchronized with the SD card or external components correctly.

Getting ready

To boot your device, you need the following ingredients:

▸ A wired up Banana Pi
▸ A prepared SD card with an operating system

How to do it...

We are going to boot up and shut down the Banana Pi.

Booting up

Do the following steps to boot up your Banana Pi:

1. Attach the Ethernet cable to your local network.
2. Connect your Banana Pi to a display.
3. Plug in an USB keyboard and mouse.
4. Insert the SD card to your device.
5. Power your Banana Pi by plugging in the USB power cable.

The following screenshot shows a new Android installation on the Banana Pi after a successful boot:

The next screenshot shows the desktop of Raspbian after a successful boot:

Shutting down Android

To shut down Android, press and hold down the Power key of the Banana Pi.

Shutting down Linux

To shut down your Linux-based distribution, you either use the `shutdown` command or do it via the desktop environment (in case of Raspbian, it is called LXDE). For the latter method, these are the steps:

1. Click on the LXDE icon in the lower-left corner.

2. Click on **Logout**.

3. Click on **Shutdown** in the upcoming window.

To shut down your operating system via the shell, type in the following command:

```
$ sudo shutdown -h now
```

How it works...

When you have prepared the SD card successfully, you can finally boot up your Banana Pi with your desired operating system.

The boot sequence should initiate immediately. You will see blinking LEDs. If only the red LED is lit, you probably made a mistake when writing the image to the SD card or the SD card is defective.

If you powered off the device previously, you may need to press and hold the Power key to restart the booting of your device. You will see the boot messages, if you connected your Banana Pi to a display. When the boot has finished, you are welcomed by your operating system for the first time.

 If you are using the wired Ethernet network interface on Android, make sure to enable **Use Ethernet** in the Android settings under **Wireless & Networks | More**.

On Linux, you can shut down the device via the shell. If you are on the desktop, you can access the shell via an application called Terminal (or LXTerminal in case of Raspbian).

The `shutdown` command expects a `mode` parameter (`-h`, that is, halt in this case) and a time (`now`). If you want to reboot your device, you can use the mode `-r` (reboot). As the `shutdown` command requires root privileges, we are executing the `shutdown` command with the prefix command `sudo`. This will issue the next command—shutdown—to be executed with root privileges. You will have to enter the password of the user. On most of the Banana Pi distributions, the default passwords for the default user is `bananapi`.

Alternatively, you can also power off or reboot your Banana Pi via the LXDE menu or the appropriate commands. The following are the commands for power off and reboot respectively:

```
$ sudo poweroff
$ sudo reboot
```

See also

- For the manual page of the `shutdown` command, use:

  ```
  $ man shutdown
  ```

- Refer to Wikipedia for the article on the `sudo` command at https://en.wikipedia.org/wiki/Sudo

2
Administration

This chapter will cover the following recipes:

- ▶ Determining the IP address and hostname
- ▶ Connecting via SSH on Windows using PuTTY
- ▶ Connecting via SSH on Unix-like systems
- ▶ User maintenance
- ▶ Searching, installing, and removing the software
- ▶ Updating the operating system
- ▶ Wireless network on the Banana Pro

Introduction

In this chapter, we will get to know the tricks of administrating the Banana Pi. Administration can be a difficult task as a lot of factors must be considered. However, we will go along this journey step by step. We will begin this chapter by connecting to the Banana Pi via a remote shell. This way, you will be able to administrate the Banana Pi from another computer on your local network. You will see that it will become a very convenient way of working with the device. You will not have to attach a keyboard and display directly to the Banana Pi anymore. Fortunately, the very basic service (that is the OpenSSH server) is configured on almost all Linux-based distributions for the Banana Pi by default. Therefore, you will only need to install and configure an SSH client onto your computer to connect to your Banana Pi remotely.

Determining the IP address and hostname

To connect to your Banana Pi via your local area network, you will need to know the IP address or the hostname of your device.

This recipe shows you how to find out the IP address and hostname of your Banana Pi.

Getting ready

The following components are required for this recipe:

- A Banana Pi running a Linux system connected to your local network
- A configured SD card containing a Linux distribution
- A keyboard, mouse, and display attached to your Banana Pi

How to do it...

Perform the following steps to determine the IP address:

1. Initiate the booting of your Banana Pi and wait for the desktop to appear.
2. Start a terminal application such as LXTerminal.
3. Type in the following `ifconfig` command:

    ```
    $ ifconfig eth0
    ```

    This will output all the information of your Ethernet device (eth0), including the IP address, subnet mask, MAC address, and some additional information. The IP address is the value after `inet addr:XXX.XXX.XXX.XXX` (for example, 192.168.0.2).

Do not confuse `inet addr` (IPv4) with `inet6 addr` (IPv6). In the following recipes, we are going to work with the IPv4 address only.

You can also find out the assigned IP address of your Banana Pi using your router configuration utility.

To determine the hostname of your Banana Pi, type in the following `hostname` command:

```
$ hostname
```

You can also identify the hostname of your Banana Pi by looking at the beginning of the command line—you see `bananapi@lemaker` by default (`bananapi` is the user and `lemaker` is the hostname).

In the next screenshot, you see the output of the `ifconfig` command and the `hostname` command:

```
bananapi@lemaker ~ $ ifconfig eth0
eth0      Link encap:Ethernet  HWaddr 02:05:04:80:f6:b0
          inet addr:192.168.178.37  Bcast:192.168.178.255  Mask:255.255.255.0
          inet6 addr: fe80::5:4ff:fe80:f6b0/64 Scope:Link
          UP BROADCAST RUNNING MULTICAST  MTU:1500  Metric:1
          RX packets:299 errors:0 dropped:0 overruns:0 frame:0
          TX packets:235 errors:0 dropped:0 overruns:0 carrier:0
          collisions:0 txqueuelen:1000
          RX bytes:28645 (27.9 KiB)  TX bytes:39482 (38.5 KiB)
          Interrupt:117 Base address:0xc000

bananapi@lemaker ~ $ hostname
lemaker
bananapi@lemaker ~ $
```

Looking at the previous screenshot, you see the IP address `192.168.178.37` is assigned to the Banana Pi by the router. We are going to use that IP address to connect to the Banana Pi via SSH in the next recipes.

You have just determined the IP address and the hostname of your Banana Pi.

How it works...

The `ifconfig` command is a utility to configure a network interface manually. You have a variety of possible parameters that you can use with `ifconfig`. Anyway, if you execute `ifconfig` without any parameters, it will output a list of information about all network interfaces that are known by your system. If you enter `ifconfig` followed by the name of the adapter, just like we did, then you see the information for this interface only.

Also, you do not necessarily need the actual IP address of your Banana Pi as every device that is connected to your network also has a hostname, which identifies the device via a name besides an IP address. You can identify the hostname of your Banana Pi by either looking at the beginning of the command line or using the `hostname` command. Thus, you are able to connect to your Banana Pi via the hostname `lemaker` or the IP address in the following recipes, if your router supports the resolution of the hostname to the IP address of its clients.

21

There's more...

We are using a terminal application to enter the previous commands. A terminal provides a **command-line interface** (**CLI**). In the case of Linux systems, the CLI is named shell. It gives us direct access to the programs and services of our operating system. There are a lot of shell implementations on the market. The default shell on most Unix-like operating systems these days is the so-called **Bourne again shell** (**Bash**).

> Bash has a feature called autocompletion. Try pressing the *Tab* key after starting to write a command. For example, if you press *Tab* after entering ifco, the Bash will complete it to the desired ifconfig command.

To extract only the IP address information (including broadcast and subnet mask), you can extend the ifconfig command with the following:

```
$ ifconfig eth0 | grep "inet addr"
```

```
bananapi@lemaker ~ $ ifconfig eth0 | grep "inet addr"
          inet addr:192.168.178.37  Bcast:192.168.178.255  Mask:255.255.255.0
bananapi@lemaker ~ $ █
```

Using the vertical line—the so-called pipe—we forward the whole output of the ifconfig command to another program called grep. Piping is a powerful way of combining different commands. It works by redirecting the standard output (stdout) from one command to the standard input (stdin) of another command—just like a real pipeline transporting oil from one end to another. The standard output is the text that is presented in the shell after issuing the command without any redirection. On the other hand, a command normally reads its input from the standard input. Piping is the solution for connecting these concepts to each other.

Grep is a powerful tool used to search for text lines (strings) within files or from the standard input (like in our example). So we let grep search for a line containing the string inet addr from the stdin, which comes from stdout of ifconfig redirected by the pipe sign.

Connecting via SSH on Windows using PuTTY

The following recipe shows you how to connect to your Banana Pi remotely using an open source application called PuTTY.

Getting ready

For this recipe, you will need the following ingredients:

▶ A booted up Linux operating system on your Banana Pi connected to your local network

▶ The PuTTY application on your Windows PC that is also connected to your local area network

How to do it...

To connect to your Banana Pi via SSH on Windows, perform the following:

1. Run `putty.exe`.

2. You will see the **PuTTY Configuration** dialog.

3. Enter the IP address of the Banana Pi and leave the **Port** as number `22` as shown in the following screenshot:

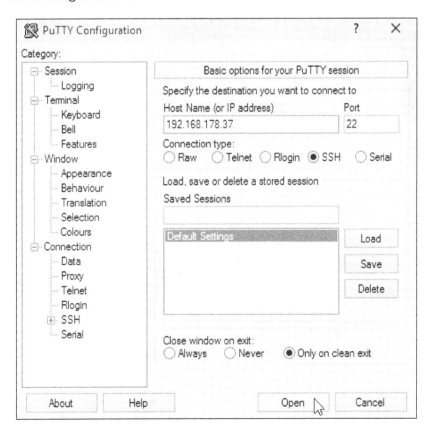

In the previous screenshot, we use the destination IP address of the Banana Pi, which we determined in the last recipe. Indeed, you need the correct IP address or hostname of your Banana Pi.

 Some routers that support DHCP have an address reservation feature. This way, you can assign your desired IP address to your Banana Pi forever.

4. Click on the **Open** button. A new terminal will appear, attempting a connection to the Banana Pi.

5. When connecting to the Banana Pi for the first time, you will see a PuTTY security alert. The following screenshot shows the **PuTTY Security Alert** window:

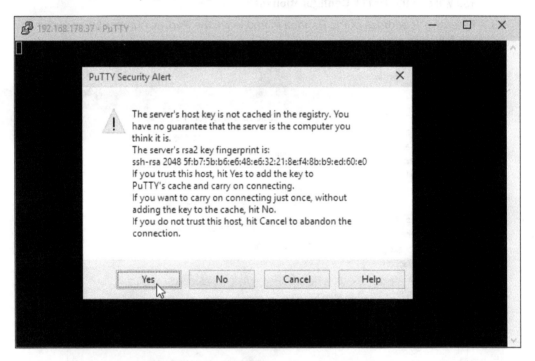

6. Trust the connection by clicking on **Yes**.

7. You will be requested to enter the login credentials. Use the default username `bananapi` and password `bananapi`.

When you are done, you should be welcomed by the shell of your Banana Pi. The following screenshot shows the shell of your Banana Pi accessed via SSH using PuTTY on Windows:

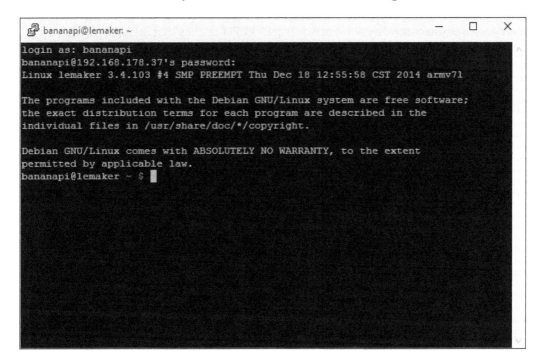

To quit your SSH session, execute the command `exit` or press *Ctrl + D*.

How it works...

PuTTY is an open source terminal emulator (tty) that handles several network protocols, including SSH and Telnet. The Telnet protocol was designed at the end of the year 1960 to provide an interactive remote terminal over a TCP connection. However, Telnet does not have any encryption implemented. Every kind of information is sent over an unencrypted channel (including user login data). Therefore, it is vulnerable to a lot of attacks over networks, in particular, from the Internet.

This is what the **SSH** (**secure shell**) protocol is solving. SSH is also a network protocol to provide remote connections to a virtual terminal. In contrast to Telnet, every kind of transmitted and received information is encrypted. This is why it is named secure shell.

There's more...

You have several options when downloading PuTTY from its website, either you just download `putty.exe` or you choose a ZIP file containing all PuTTY utilities that are offered. Also, an installer is available on that website. I recommend selecting the ZIP file that also contains the PuTTYgen application, which we are going to use in a later recipe when improving the security by using SSH keys.

Furthermore, you can save the hostname or IP address, including the username to be chosen, as a so-called saved session in the PuTTY configuration. Here are the steps:

1. Navigate to **Connection** | **Data** on the right-hand side of the **Category** option.
2. Enter the desired username (`bananapi` by default) into the auto-login username text field.
3. Switch back to **Session** on the right **Category** side.
4. Enter the hostname or IP address into the appropriate text field.
5. Enter an arbitrary name for your saved session into the text field beneath **Saved Sessions**.
6. Click on **Save**.

This way you can access your Banana Pi conveniently the next time you start PuTTY by double-clicking on the name of your saved session.

If you install a new image to your Banana Pi, a new SSH server key is generated or included usually. This means, you will see a new security warning when trying to connect to a newly installed Banana Pi. If you have already reinstalled your Banana Pi, you can ignore this warning by clicking on **Yes**.

See also

▶ PuTTY is a free client for Telnet and SSH for Windows (and Unix) platforms. For more information on this, go to `http://www.chiark.greenend.org.uk/~sgtatham/putty/`.

Connecting via SSH on Unix-like systems

In this recipe, we will connect to the Banana Pi using SSH on Linux or other Unix-like operating systems such as Mac OS X or FreeBSD. You probably have installed the required OpenSSH client already.

Getting ready

You will need the following ingredients to connect to your Banana Pi using SSH:

- ▸ A booted up Linux operating system on your Banana Pi connected to your local network
- ▸ A PC or Mac running a Unix-like operating system that has the OpenSSH client installed and is also connected to your local area network

How to do it...

To connect to your Banana Pi, you only need to perform the following steps:

1. Open an arbitrary terminal program of your operating system.

2. Type in the following `ssh` command into your shell:

   ```
   $ ssh -l bananapi 192.168.178.37
   ```

    In the previous command, we use the destination IP address of the Banana Pi, which we determined earlier. Indeed, you need the correct IP address or hostname of your Banana Pi.

3. When trying to connect for the first time, you will be prompted to trust the yet unrecognized SSH server key at first. In this case, type `yes` to trust the server and hit *Enter*.

4. You will be requested to enter the password of the user `bananapi` that is also `bananapi` by default.

Afterwards, you will see the shell of your Banana Pi on your terminal application.

The following screenshot shows an SSH login to the Banana Pi from a Linux PC running the `xfce4-terminal` terminal application:

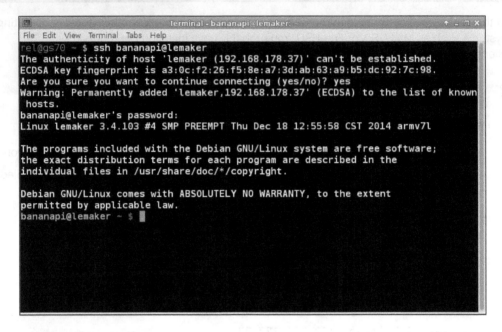

How it works...

On most Unix-like systems, you are able to connect to remote SSH servers by default, as the required SSH client program is often already installed.

That program requires at least a destination IP address or hostname. We prepend the `-l` (login) parameter to choose a desired user for the login. If you do not enter a user to login, the local user that is currently trying to run the command will be chosen (`rel` in the previous screenshot).

As you can see in the previous screenshot, you can also shorten the command by typing the following command:

```
$ ssh username@host
```

There's more...

Most SSH client installations on Unix-like operating systems are able to read an optional configuration file to apply parameters to a desired host. If you append the following configuration to the file ~/.ssh/config (which will need to be created if not already existing), you can connect to your Banana Pi easily via ssh banana.

```
Host banana
    HostName 192.168.178.37
    User bananapi
```

As always, you need to replace the IP address after HostName with the correct IP address of the Banana Pi or the hostname. You can choose the name after Host (banana in the previous example) as you like. If you have more than one host configured, each name must be unique. Also, you can append a lot more parameters to the host configuration.

See also

▸ The manual pages of the default SSH client on most Unix-like systems and its configuration:

```
$ man ssh
$ man ssh_config
```

User maintenance

Most Linux distributions for the Banana Pi come preconfigured with a default username and password. The login information is published on the download website for the operating system images (see *Chapter 1, Installation and Setup*).

In almost all cases, the credentials are:

Username	Password
bananapi	bananapi

You might want to create your own user on the system. At the very least, it is highly recommended you change the default password of the default user. This recipe explains the necessary tasks.

Getting ready

The following ingredients are required to create or delete users and to change their passwords:

- ▸ A booted up Linux operating system on your Banana Pi
- ▸ SSH connection if you plan to do the user maintenance remotely; however, in most of the upcoming recipes, you can do the user maintenance directly on Banana Pi

How to do it...

We will split this recipe into adding a user, changing a password, and deleting a user.

Adding a new user

We are going to use the `useradd` and the `passwd` commands to add a new user with the name `alice` and the password `wonderland`. Choose any other name and password as you wish.

1. Connect to your Banana Pi remotely or open a terminal on the desktop.

2. Type in the following command to add a new user alice:

   ```
   $ sudo useradd -m -s /bin/bash alice
   ```

3. If you are requested to type the password for `sudo`, enter the default password, that is, `bananapi`.

4. Now, we want to add the new user to all the groups that the default user is a member of. To do so, we have to find out the groups of our default user:

   ```
   $ groups
   ```

5. We get a list of all groups of the `bananapi` user. To assign alice to these groups, we use the following command:

   ```
   $ sudo usermod -a -G
   pi,adm,dialout,cdrom,sudo,audio,video,plugdev,games,users,
   netdev,input,indiecity,spi,gpio alice
   ```

   Keep in mind, that the groups are separated by a comma and not a space. Also note that depending on your distribution, the list of groups may differ.

You have just created a new user name `alice` and assigned the user to all groups that the default `bananapi` user is a member of.

Setting a password for a user

Now we are setting a password for our new user alice:

1. Type the following command to give the new user a password:

    `$ sudo passwd alice`

2. You will be requested to type the desired password. Enter the password `wonderland`.

3. Repeat the password `wonderland`.

4. The command will reply with: `passwd: password updated successfully`.

You have assigned the password `wonderland` to the user alice. Take a look at the following screenshot:

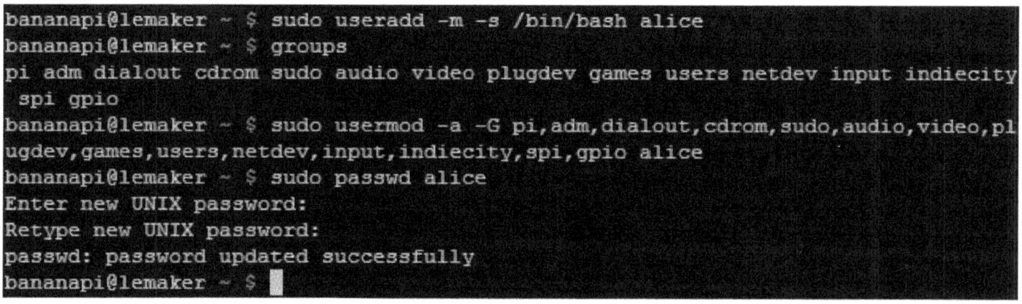

```
bananapi@lemaker ~ $ sudo useradd -m -s /bin/bash alice
bananapi@lemaker ~ $ groups
pi adm dialout cdrom sudo audio video plugdev games users netdev input indiecity
 spi gpio
bananapi@lemaker ~ $ sudo usermod -a -G pi,adm,dialout,cdrom,sudo,audio,video,pl
ugdev,games,users,netdev,input,indiecity,spi,gpio alice
bananapi@lemaker ~ $ sudo passwd alice
Enter new UNIX password:
Retype new UNIX password:
passwd: password updated successfully
bananapi@lemaker ~ $
```

In the preceding screenshot, you see the adding of the user, the group assignment, and the password assignment of the user alice.

Deleting a user

To delete the previously created user, we use the `userdel` command:

1. Type the following command into a shell to delete the user alice:

    `$ sudo userdel alice`

2. If you are requested to enter a password for `sudo`, use the default password `bananapi`

You have successfully deleted the user alice.

How it works...

Linux and other Unix-like operating systems are so-called multiuser systems. The name implies that these systems are able to handle more than one user simultaneously. Each user has its very own place where their files and configurations belong, the so-called home directory (often abbreviated as ~).

Most user modifications require root privileges. Therefore, we prefix every command with sudo.

We are adding a new user by executing the useradd command. This command takes some parameters. The -m parameter will tell useradd to create the home directory automatically (/home/alice in our case). As the new user wants to be able to log in, we have to set a default shell, which is done by -s followed by the full path to the shell (the path to Bash in our example). Last but not least, the user must have a name, which is alice in our previous case.

Also, a user can be assigned to different groups, which have different permissions for various tasks. To find out which groups are assigned to the default user, we are using the groups command. When executed, it outputs all groups of the current user (that is bananapi). We assign the same groups to our user alice by using the usermod (user modify) command. The usermod command modifies information about a user, -a in combination with -G adds the user to a so-called *supplementary group*, which is given as a comma-separated list.

Since each user should have a password, we assign a password by using the passwd command. You can also change the password of the default user bananapi this way.

Finally, if we want to delete a user, we simply issue the userdel command.

There's more...

If you delete a user by the userdel command, the user's home directory will remain untouched. Thus, if you also want to delete their whole home directory, you will need to use the rm (remove) command forcing (-f) and recursive (-r):

```
$ sudo rm -rf /home/alice
```

 The rm -rf command will remove the whole directory that you issued without any confirmation. So use that command with absolute care, as you can easily remove the wrong folder or even destroy the system!

Another interesting command is the id command. It provides additional information such as user ID (uid) and the user's associated group IDs (gid). The following screenshot shows group information for the user alice by issuing the id command:

```
bananapi@lemaker ~ $ id
uid=1000(bananapi) gid=1000(pi) groups=1000(pi),4(adm),20(dialout),24(cdrom),27(
sudo),29(audio),44(video),46(plugdev),60(games),100(users),105(netdev),999(input
),1001(indiecity),1002(spi),1003(gpio)
```

See also

▸ A helpful article about user and group management in Arch Linux, which is also usable for most other distributions is available at `https://wiki.archlinux.org/index.php/Users_and_groups`

▸ Manual pages of `useradd`, `passwd`, `usermod`, `userdel`, `id`, and `groups`; for example:

```
$ man useradd
```

Each manual page contains informative material about these commands.

Searching, installing, and removing the software

Once you have your decent operating system on the Banana Pi, sooner or later you are going to require a new software. As most software for Linux systems is published as open source, you can obtain the source code and compile it for yourself. However, this can be a difficult task and we will cover it in later recipes.

One alternative is to use a package manager. A lot of software is precompiled and provided as installable packages by the so-called repositories. In case of Debian-based distributions (for example, Raspbian, Bananian, and Lubuntu), the package manager that uses these repositories is called **Advanced Packaging Tool** (**Apt**).

The two most important tools for our requirements will be apt-get and apt-cache.

In this recipe, we will cover the searching, the installing, and removing of software using the Apt utilities.

Getting ready

The following ingredients are required for this recipe.

▸ A booted Debian-based operating system on your Banana Pi
▸ An Internet connection

How to do it...

We will separate this recipe into searching for, installing and removing of packages.

Searching for packages

In the upcoming example, we will search for a solitaire game:

1. Connect to your Banana Pi remotely or open a terminal on the desktop.

2. Type the following command into the shell:

   ```
   $ apt-cache search solitaire
   ```

3. You will get a list of packages that contain the string solitaire in their package name or description.

4. Each line represents a package and shows the package name and description separated by a dash (-).

Now we have obtained a list of solitaire games:

```
bananapi@lemaker ~ $ apt-cache search solitaire
ace-of-penguins - penguin-themed solitaire games
aisleriot - GNOME solitaire card game collection
freecell-solver-bin - Library for solving Freecell games
jester - board game similar to Othello
kmahjongg - mahjongg solitaire game
kpat - solitaire card games
kshisen - Shisen-Sho solitaire game
libfreecell-solver-dev - Library for solving Freecell games (Development files)
libfreecell-solver0 - Library for solving Freecell games
mah-jong - Original Mah-Jong game
mahjongg - classic Eastern tile game for GNOME
ncurses-examples - test programs and examples for ncurses
peg-e - peg elimination solitaire game
peg-solitaire - Board game for one player with pegs
pegsolitaire - An education game similar to Hi-Q
pysolfc - collection of more than 1000 solitaire card games
sgt-puzzles - Simon Tatham's Portable Puzzle Collection - 1-player puzzle games
vdr-plugin-solitaire - Plugin to vdr that implements the card game "Solitaire"
xmahjongg - tile-based solitaire game
xsol - Solitaire game for the X Window system
```

The preceding screenshot shows the output after searching for packages containing the string solitaire using the apt-cache command.

Installing a package

We are going to install a package by using its package name. From the previous received list, we select the package ace-of-penguins.

1. Type the following command into the shell:

   ```
   $ sudo apt-get install ace-of-penguins
   ```

2. If asked to type the password for `sudo`, enter the user's password.

3. If a package requires additional packages (dependencies), you will be asked to confirm the additional packages.

4. In this case, enter `Y`.

5. After downloading and installing, the desired package is installed:

```
bananapi@lemaker ~ $ sudo apt-get install ace-of-penguins
[sudo] password for bananapi:
Reading package lists... Done
Building dependency tree
Reading state information... Done
The following NEW packages will be installed:
  ace-of-penguins
0 upgraded, 1 newly installed, 0 to remove and 36 not upgraded.
Need to get 264 kB of archives.
After this operation, 578 kB of additional disk space will be used.
Get:1 http://mirrordirector.raspbian.org/raspbian/ wheezy/main ace-of-penguins armhf 1.3-8 [264 kB]
Fetched 264 kB in 5s (49.4 kB/s)
Selecting previously unselected package ace-of-penguins.
(Reading database ... 67876 files and directories currently installed.)
Unpacking ace-of-penguins (from .../ace-of-penguins_1.3-8_armhf.deb) ...
Processing triggers for desktop-file-utils ...
Processing triggers for hicolor-icon-theme ...
Processing triggers for menu ...
Processing triggers for man-db ...
Setting up ace-of-penguins (1.3-8) ...
Processing triggers for menu ...
bananapi@lemaker ~ $
```

The previous screenshot shows the installation process of the package `ace-of-penguins`.

 When installing the game suite `ace-of-penguins`, you will be able to play the games on your desktop only.

Removing a package

When you want to uninstall (remove) a package, you also use the `apt-get` command:

1. Type the following command into a shell:

   `$ sudo apt-get remove ace-of-penguins`

2. If asked to type the password for `sudo`, enter the user's password.

3. You will be asked to confirm the removal.

4. Enter `Y`.

5. After this process, the package is removed from your system.

You will have uninstalled the package `ace-of-penguins`.

How it works...

The `apt-cache` and `apt-get` commands use the same information that remain in the apt packages' cache. While `apt-cache` is used to query information from the cache itself, `apt-get` actually fetches packages based on this information. Moreover, `apt-get` handles dependencies. Package dependencies are supplementary packages that are required to install a specific package successfully.

As shown in the following screenshot, you can start a solitaire game by navigating to **LXPanel | Games | Penguin Solitaire**. Alternatively, you can run the game directly using the **LXTerminal** or by navigating to **LXPanel | Run** and typing the `ace-solitaire` command.

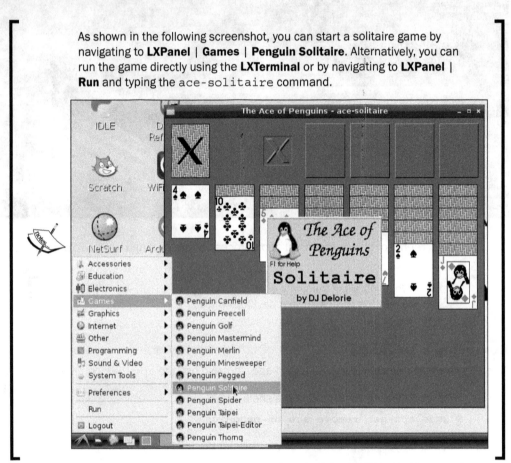

There's more...

In the case of Debian-based distributions, the packages itself are `.deb` files that are provided by the repositories and installed using the Debian tool dpkg. The best feature of Apt is its dependency resolution based on repositories and its way of interacting with dpkg without the need to use specific file names.

However, dpkg is the actual package management system on Debian-based distributions. You can install packages that you downloaded in the `.deb` file format using `dpkg -i package.deb`. By using `dpkg -l`, you can list all currently installed packages. This will output a long list, which you can filter using the pipe and `grep` trick we discussed in the *Determining the IP address and hostname* recipe. For example, consider the following command:

```
$ dpkg -l | grep solitaire
```

This will search for the string solitaire in the whole list of installed packages.

You can also find out, which files are installed by a specific package using the following command:

```
$ dpkg -L ace-of-penguins
```

In reverse, you can find out to what installed package, a specific file belongs to:

```
$ dpkg -S /usr/games/ace-solitaire
```

Furthermore, when uninstalling a package using the `remove` parameter, the configuration files you must have created in the meantime are untouched. If you want to completely uninstall anything regarding a specific package, use the `purge` parameter instead, as follows:

```
$ sudo apt-get purge ace-of-penguins
```

See also

▸ Informative wiki article from the creators of Apt at `https://wiki.debian.org/Apt`
▸ Manual page for users who wish to understand dpkg's command-line options and details:

```
$ man dpkg
```

Updating the operating system

This recipe explains how to update your Linux operating system using the apt-get program.

Updating (or *upgrading*) the Linux system is important, still quite simple. Almost every day, the community improves the software that is used on Linux systems. Some updates are just for new features while others are incredibly important. Think of the dangerous Heartbleed Bug in the widely used cryptography library OpenSSL in April 2014.

Therefore, distribution upgrading is highly recommended on a regular basis but at least once a month.

Getting ready

The following ingredients are required for this recipe:

▸ A booted Debian-based operating system on your Banana Pi

▸ An Internet connection

How to do it...

Upgrade your whole Debian-based Linux distribution by performing the following steps:

1. Connect to your Banana Pi remotely or open a terminal on the desktop.

2. Type in the following command into the shell:

   `$ sudo apt-get update`

3. If asked to type the password for `sudo`, enter the user's password.

4. Apt will now download the updated packages information from the repositories:

```
bananapi@lemaker ~ $ sudo apt-get update
Get:1 http://archive.raspberrypi.org wheezy Release.gpg [490 B]
Get:2 http://mirrordirector.raspbian.org wheezy Release.gpg [490 B]
Get:3 http://mirrordirector.raspbian.org wheezy Release [14.4 kB]
Get:4 http://archive.raspberrypi.org wheezy Release [10.2 kB]
Get:5 http://raspberrypi.collabora.com wheezy Release.gpg [836 B]
Get:6 http://raspberrypi.collabora.com wheezy Release [7,514 B]
Get:7 http://mirrordirector.raspbian.org wheezy/main armhf Packages [6,897 kB]
Get:8 http://archive.raspberrypi.org wheezy/main armhf Packages [108 kB]
Get:9 http://raspberrypi.collabora.com wheezy/rpi armhf Packages [2,214 B]
Hit http://repository.wolfram.com stable Release.gpg
Hit http://repository.wolfram.com stable Release
Hit http://repository.wolfram.com stable/non-free armhf Packages
Ign http://raspberrypi.collabora.com wheezy/rpi Translation-en_GB
Ign http://raspberrypi.collabora.com wheezy/rpi Translation-en
Ign http://archive.raspberrypi.org wheezy/main Translation-en_GB
Ign http://archive.raspberrypi.org wheezy/main Translation-en
Ign http://repository.wolfram.com stable/non-free Translation-en_GB
Ign http://repository.wolfram.com stable/non-free Translation-en
Hit http://mirrordirector.raspbian.org wheezy/contrib armhf Packages
Hit http://mirrordirector.raspbian.org wheezy/non-free armhf Packages
Hit http://mirrordirector.raspbian.org wheezy/rpi armhf Packages
Ign http://mirrordirector.raspbian.org wheezy/contrib Translation-en_GB
Ign http://mirrordirector.raspbian.org wheezy/contrib Translation-en
Ign http://mirrordirector.raspbian.org wheezy/main Translation-en_GB
Ign http://mirrordirector.raspbian.org wheezy/main Translation-en
Ign http://mirrordirector.raspbian.org wheezy/non-free Translation-en_GB
Ign http://mirrordirector.raspbian.org wheezy/non-free Translation-en
Ign http://mirrordirector.raspbian.org wheezy/rpi Translation-en_GB
Ign http://mirrordirector.raspbian.org wheezy/rpi Translation-en
Fetched 7,041 kB in 19s (362 kB/s)
Reading package lists... Done
```

5. We are going to actually upgrade our system by entering the following command:

    ```
    $ sudo apt-get dist-upgrade
    ```

6. Apt will calculate the upgrade; this might take a few seconds/minutes.

7. A list of upgradable packages is presented; continue by entering Y:

```
bananapi@lemaker ~ $ sudo apt-get dist-upgrade
Reading package lists... Done
Building dependency tree
Reading state information... Done
Calculating upgrade... Done
The following packages will be REMOVED:
  libfm-gtk-bin libfm-gtk1 libfm1
The following NEW packages will be installed:
  init-system-helpers libfm-extra4 libfm-gtk-data libfm-gtk4 libfm-modules
  libfm4 libpng12-dev libqt4-network libssh-4 lxpanel-data
The following packages will be upgraded:
  apt apt-utils base-files bash ca-certificates cpio cups-bsd cups-client
  cups-common curl dbus dbus-x11 dosfstools e2fslibs e2fsprogs fake-hwclock
  file firmware-brcm80211 gnome-themes-standard-data gnupg gpgv krb5-locales
  libapt-inst1.5 libapt-pkg-dev libapt-pkg4.12 libarchive12 libavcodec53
  libavutil51 libc-bin libc-dev-bin libc6 libc6-dev libcomerr2 libcups2
  libcupsimage2 libcurl3 libcurl3-gnutls libdbus-1-3 libevent-2.0-5 libflac8
  libfm-data libfreetype6 libfreetype6-dev libgcrypt11 libgssapi-krb5-2
  libjasper1 libjavascriptcoregtk-3.0-0 libk5crypto3 libkeyutils1 libkrb5-3
  libkrb5support0 libmagic1 libpixman-1-0 libsmbclient libss2 libssh2-1
  libssl1.0.0 libtasn1-3 libwbclient0 libwebkitgtk-3.0-0
  libwebkitgtk-3.0-common libxml2 libyaml-0-2 locales lxpanel mime-support
  multiarch-support ntp omxplayer openssl pcmanfm perl perl-base perl-modules
  raspberrypi-artwork raspi-config rsyslog samba-common smbclient sonic-pi
  sudo tzdata unzip wget wpagui wpasupplicant xdg-utils xserver-common
  xserver-xorg-core
89 upgraded, 10 newly installed, 3 to remove and 0 not upgraded.
Need to get 109 MB of archives.
After this operation, 24.4 MB of additional disk space will be used.
Do you want to continue [Y/n]?
```

8. The new packages are downloaded and will upgrade the existing ones. This might take some time.

You have successfully upgraded your Linux system.

How it works...

To upgrade the system's software packages, Apt uses the currently available information about all the packages that are in Apt's cache. To upgrade the system with current software, we need to update this information beforehand.

Therefore, we are using the `update` parameter for apt-get to issue the downloading of the updated package information.

Later on, Apt is informed about the new available software on the repositories. We will install the updates via the `dist-upgrade` (distribution upgrade) parameter for `apt-get`.

There's more...

Sometimes when upgrading packages, old dependency packages are not required any more—they become deprecated. To automatically remove packages that are not needed anymore, you can use the `autoremove` parameter for `apt-get`:

```
$ sudo apt-get autoremove
```

When upgraded packages are installed, the old packages may remain in your downloaded local repository. To clean these obsolete packages from your filesystem, you can use the `autoclean` parameter:

```
$ sudo apt-get autoclean
```

Upgrading packages often includes upgrading system configuration files. We are going to modify configuration files in the upcoming recipes. Therefore, it is possible that dpkg detects a so-called configuration file modification.

This means an upgradable configuration file, that you modified previously, is not in the default state anymore. You will be prompted on how to proceed. In most cases, you want to keep your changes to the configuration file. Therefore, you should enter N (to keep the currently-installed version) in most cases, as shown in the following screenshot:

```
Configuration file `/etc/bash.bashrc'
 ==> Modified (by you or by a script) since installation.
 ==> Package distributor has shipped an updated version.
   What would you like to do about it ?  Your options are:
    Y or I  : install the package maintainer's version
    N or O  : keep your currently-installed version
      D     : show the differences between the versions
      Z     : start a shell to examine the situation
 The default action is to keep your current version.
*** bash.bashrc (Y/I/N/O/D/Z) [default=N] ? n
```

However, sometimes new configuration options are shipped with upgraded packages or old configuration options become deprecated. It is recommended that you check the newly provided configuration file that is installed besides the configuration file you have saved with the `.dpkg-dist` file extension (`/etc/bash.bashrc.dpkg-dist` in the previous case).

You can avoid the configuration file prompt by issuing `apt-get` with the following dpkg options:

```
$ sudo apt-get -o Dpkg::Options::="--force-confdef" -o
Dpkg::Options::="--force-confold" dist-upgrade
```

Also, you can make these options permanent. Create a file `/etc/apt/apt.conf.d/local` with root privileges containing:

```
Dpkg::Options {
    "--force-confdef";
    "--force-confold";
}
```

Wireless network on the Banana Pro

This recipe explains how to configure a wireless network on the Banana Pro.

Getting ready

The following ingredients are required for this recipe.

- A Banana Pro with the wireless LAN antenna attached
- An SD card containing the Raspbian operating system for the Banana Pro
- An attached keyboard, mouse, and display to configure WLAN via the desktop
- Alternatively, an SSH connection to configure WLAN manually

To attach the WLAN antenna, flip your Banana Pro, and carefully plug in the antenna into its slot beneath the Micro SD slot. The following image shows the Banana Pro and the wireless LAN antenna plugged in correctly:

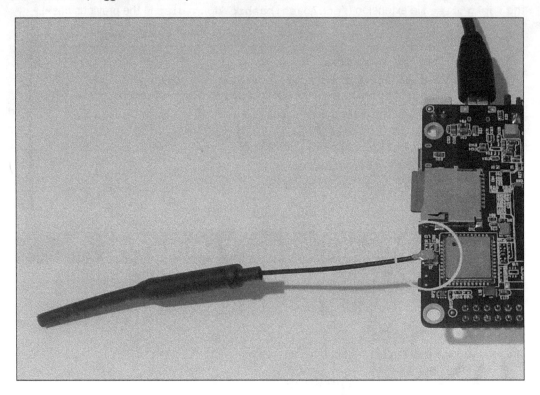

How to do it...

We need to do two things to configure the wireless network.

Loading the ap6210 module

The wireless LAN interface depends on a special module named ap6210. The following are the steps to load this module:

1. Open a shell.

2. Load the module by typing:

    ```
    $ sudo modprobe ap6210
    ```

3. Type the following command to list all the currently loaded modules:

    ```
    $ lsmod
    ```

4. Besides some other modules, you should see the module `ap6210`:

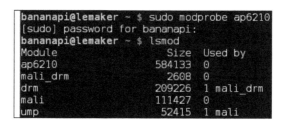

```
bananapi@lemaker ~ $ sudo modprobe ap6210
[sudo] password for bananapi:
bananapi@lemaker ~ $ lsmod
Module                    Size  Used by
ap6210                  584133  0
mali_drm                  2608  0
drm                     209226  1 mali_drm
mali                    111427  0
ump                      52415  1 mali
```

The correct module is loaded if you see `ap6210` in the list of loaded modules, as shown in the preceding screenshot. To load the `ap6210` module automatically on system boot, perform the following steps:

1. Open a shell

2. Type the following command:

   `$ sudo -s`

3. You get a root shell

4. Append the string `ap6210` to `/etc/modules`:

   `# echo ap6210 >> /etc/modules`

 Make sure to use the greater than symbol twice (`>>`). Otherwise you will overwrite `/etc/modules`.

5. Quit the root shell by using the `exit` command or *Ctrl + D*.

The `ap6210` module should be loaded on booting from now on.

Configuring the wireless network with WiFi Config

To configure the wireless network on the desktop, you can use the application WiFi Config. It is a tool that is simple and straight forward. And here is how to do it:

1. Once the Banana Pro is booted up, open WiFi Config on the desktop.

2. Make sure **Adapter wlan0** is selected.

3. Click on the **Manage Networks** tab.

4. Now, click on the **Scan** button to scan the available networks.

5. Click on **Close** to close the Scan results.

6. Click on the **Add** button.

7. A new window with the title **NetworkConfig** appears.

8. Enter the credentials for your wireless network:

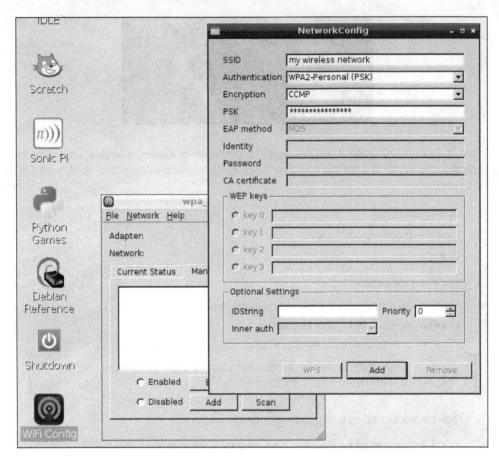

9. Click on **Add**.

10. Your wireless configuration is shown within the list on **Manage Networks** and will be selected in as the **Network** beneath **Adapter**.

11. Click on the **Current Status** tab.

12. The Banana Pro should be connected to your access point and should show you the connection details.

Your Banana Pro is connected to your wireless LAN if you see an assigned IP address as shown in the following screenshot:

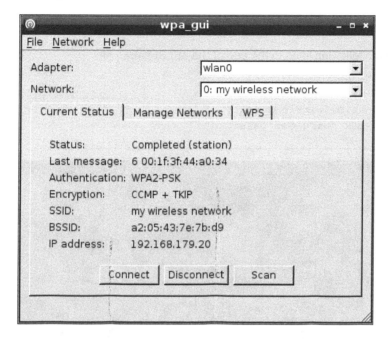

Configuring the wireless network manually

If you want to configure your WLAN manually on the shell, you need to perform the following steps:

 If you configured your WLAN previously using the WiFi Config tool, firstly, remove your network from the list in the **Manage Network** list.

1. Open a shell.
2. Change to the directory `/etc/network`:

   `$ cd /etc/network/`

3. Create a backup of the current `interfaces` file to be safe:

   `$ sudo cp interfaces interfaces.backup`

4. Edit the `interfaces` file using a text editor like nano:

   `$ sudo nano interfaces`

5. Remove or comment out the following lines from the `interfaces` file:

```
allow-hotplug wlan0
iface wlan0 inet manual
wpa-roam /etc/wpa_supplicant/wpa_supplicant.conf
```

6. Add the following lines to the end of the `interfaces` file:

```
auto wlan0
iface wlan0 inet dhcp
   wpa-ssid "wireless_ssid"
   wpa-psk "wireless_password"
```

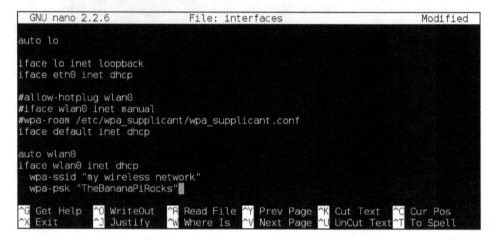

```
GNU nano 2.2.6                  File: interfaces                    Modified

auto lo

iface lo inet loopback
iface eth0 inet dhcp

#allow-hotplug wlan0
#iface wlan0 inet manual
#wpa-roam /etc/wpa_supplicant/wpa_supplicant.conf
iface default inet dhcp

auto wlan0
iface wlan0 inet dhcp
   wpa-ssid "my wireless network"
   wpa-psk "TheBananaPiRocks"█

^G Get Help   ^O WriteOut   ^R Read File  ^Y Prev Page  ^K Cut Text   ^C Cur Pos
^X Exit       ^J Justify    ^W Where Is   ^V Next Page  ^U UnCut Text ^T To Spell
```

 Use your SSID and WPA key of your wireless network as values enclosed by double quotes for the options `wpa-ssid` and `wpa-psk`.

7. Exit the nano editor by pressing *Ctrl + X*.

8. Confirm the modifications with the *Y* key.

9. Press the *Enter* key to confirm the filename `interfaces`.

10. You will be redirected back to the shell.

11. Restart the Banana Pro by entering the following command:

```
$ sudo shutdown -r now
```

If everything is entered correctly, your wireless network adapter should work now. You are able to see the current status by executing `ifconfig wlan0`.

How it works...

While a lot of devices on your Linux computer work out-of-the-box as the necessary drivers are included in the **kernel**, other devices do not. A kernel is the central core of your operating system handling processes, organizing files, accessing the hardware, and so forth. On our Banana Pi, the kernel is named Linux. The Linux kernel is fortunately able to load hardware drivers dynamically in the form of so-called, modules while running.

A kernel module is a piece of code containing, for example, the necessary driver for a WLAN adapter. In the case of the Banana Pro, the driver is included in a module named ap6210.

To load a kernel module, you use the **modprobe** (probe module) command, which requires root privileges. To list all the currently loaded modules, you can use the lsmod (list modules) command. To persist the loading of a module, you can add the module name into /etc/ modules. With the echo ap6210 >> /etc/modules command, we output the string ap6210 via the echo command. However, instead of outputting the string to the shell, we direct the output to /etc/modules. As we want to append the string to the existing file, we use the greater than sign twice. If we used it once, we would overwrite the file, which is dangerous as other relevant modules of the Banana Pi are already configured there.

Once the required driver module is loaded successfully, we can configure the wireless network interface. You can configure WLAN the easy way using the desktop application WiFi Config, or manually using the shell.

While using the WiFi Config utility, the configuration is straight forward and self-explanatory; the manual configuration might require further explanation.

On Debian-based distributions, the network interfaces are normally configured using the system file /etc/network/interfaces. Within that file, you will also find the configuration for the loopback and Ethernet interface.

We changed the working directory from the default home directory to /etc/network using the cd (change directory) command. Then we created a backup of the existing interfaces file by the cp (copy) command. As /etc/network is a system directory, you require root privileges to modify contents of this directory (by prefixing the commands with sudo).

The default wireless LAN configuration is an appropriate choice for the WiFi Config tool, which is a frontend of a utility called wpa_supplicant. As we want to configure our WLAN interface manually, we need to remove or comment out the existing configuration options regarding the WLAN device. Commenting out means to prefix a line of a configuration option with the hash key (#). When a line is commented out, it will be ignored. In the preceding screenshot, you can see that we did not remove the lines, but commented them out to leave us with the option of simply uncommenting them, if we want to restore the default configuration in the future.

There's more...

Since all users on your Banana Pi are able to read the file `/etc/network/interfaces`, it might be a good idea to obfuscate your wireless password (the WPA passphrase). To do so, you can use the `wpa_passphrase` command as follows:

```
$ wpa_passphrase "my wireless network" "TheBananaPiRocks"
```

The first parameter has to be the SSID of your WLAN access point, the second parameter the WPA password.

The command will output something like this:

```
network={
  ssid="my wireless network"
  #psk="TheBananaPiRocks"
  psk=c0700763a5 … 7ea72bc4df
}
```

You can use the long hexadecimal value after `psk=` as the value for `wpa-psk` in `/etc/network/interfaces`. The following screenshot shows the WPA passphrase obfuscated in the `interfaces` file:

```
auto wlan0
iface wlan0 inet dhcp
  wpa-ssid "my wireless network"
  wpa-psk c0700763a5b29df7805d384877db846a72e1dc021bce7167f6e9d97ea72bc4df
```

While loading the modules executing the `modprobe` command, you are also able to unload a module using the `rmmod` (remove module) command:

```
$ sudo rmmod ap6210
```

Of course, this will disable the WLAN feature. If you append `ap6210` into the `/etc/modules` system configuration file, it will be reloaded on reboot. In this case, you will open the file `/etc/modules` with a text editor, such as nano, with root privileges and remove or uncomment the line `ap6210`.

3
External Disks

In this chapter, we will cover the following recipes:

- ▶ Mounting a USB drive
- ▶ Mounting an SSD or HDD via SATA
- ▶ Mounting via fstab
- ▶ Booting from an external disk

Introduction

This chapter is all about external disk drives. We will connect and mount USB drives and HDD or SSD drives using the SATA connector. Furthermore, we are going to explore the possibility of moving the root filesystem to, and booting from, an external drive.

Mounting a USB drive

USB flash drives are widely used to store various files and directories. They are great to exchange data from or to different computers. They are found literally everywhere. In this recipe, we are going to mount an external USB flash drive. This way, you will have access to the contents of the flash drives.

Getting ready

This recipe requires the following ingredients:

- ▶ A booted up Linux on the Banana Pi
- ▶ A USB flash drive
- ▶ Access to the Banana Pi's shell

How to do it...

Perform the following to successfully mount a USB flash drive (also called USB disk):

1. Boot up your Linux distribution on the Banana Pi.

2. Attach the USB flash drive to one of the available USB ports, as shown in the following image:

 On some distributions (such as Raspbian), the USB drive may be mounted automatically by a program called `udisks`.

3. Determine the USB device by entering the following command into a shell:

```
$ sudo fdisk -l
```

4. You will see a list of attached disks. The following screenshot shows the output of the `fdisk -l` command:

```
bananapi@lemaker ~ $ sudo fdisk -l
[sudo] password for bananapi:

Disk /dev/sda: 16.3 GB, 16307384320 bytes
60 heads, 24 sectors/track, 22118 cylinders, total 31850360 sectors
Units = sectors of 1 * 512 = 512 bytes
Sector size (logical/physical): 512 bytes / 512 bytes
I/O size (minimum/optimal): 512 bytes / 512 bytes
Disk identifier: 0xe1bbef84

   Device Boot      Start         End      Blocks   Id  System
/dev/sda1            2048    31850359    15924156    b  W95 FAT32

Disk /dev/mmcblk0: 7948 MB, 7948206080 bytes
4 heads, 16 sectors/track, 242560 cylinders, total 15523840 sectors
Units = sectors of 1 * 512 = 512 bytes
Sector size (logical/physical): 512 bytes / 512 bytes
I/O size (minimum/optimal): 512 bytes / 512 bytes
Disk identifier: 0x00090806

     Device Boot      Start       End      Blocks   Id  System
/dev/mmcblk0p1         8192    122879       57344    c  W95 FAT32 (LBA)
/dev/mmcblk0p2       122880   6399999     3138560   83  Linux
```

5. Type the following command to see whether the USB drive is currently mounted:

   `$ mount | grep sda`

6. If you get a result the same as in the following screenshot, your flash drive is already mounted:

```
bananapi@lemaker ~ $ mount | grep sda
/dev/sda1 on /media/USB_FLASH type vfat (rw,nosuid,nodev,relatime,uid=1000,gid=1
000,fmask=0022,dmask=0077,codepage=cp437,iocharset=ascii,shortname=mixed,showexe
c,utf8,flush,errors=remount-ro,uhelper=udisks)
```

7. If you get a result similar to the previous screenshot, you could use the USB drive already mounted. However, we will go on by unmounting it:

   `$ sudo umount /dev/sda1`

8. Create a target directory to mount the USB disk into:

   `$ sudo mkdir /media/usb_drive`

9. Mount the first partition of the USB disk into that directory:

   `$ sudo mount -o umask=000 /dev/sda1 /media/usb_drive`

10. You have mounted the USB disk.

11. List the contents of the USB drive:

```
$ ls -la /media/usb_drive
```

```
bananapi@lemaker ~ $ sudo mkdir /media/usb_drive
bananapi@lemaker ~ $ sudo mount -o umask=000 /dev/sda1 /media/usb_drive
bananapi@lemaker ~ $ ls -la /media/usb_drive
total 36
drwxrwxrwx 4 root root 8192 Jan  1  1970 .
drwxr-xr-x 3 root root 4096 Mar 14 07:29 ..
drwxrwxrwx 2 root root 8192 Mar 14 07:27 another directory
-rwxrwxrwx 1 root root   15 Mar 14 07:27 hello_world.txt
drwxrwxrwx 2 root root 8192 Mar 14 07:27 hide directory
```

You have mounted the USB disk successfully. In the previous screenshot, you can see the creation of the mounting destination directory, the mounting itself and the list of all contents on the USB drive.

How it works...

In this recipe, we are attaching a USB drive to a USB slot on the Banana Pi. To make the contents of an external drive for the Banana Pi available, we need to mount the drive. By mounting a drive, its filesystem will become accessible for input/output (I/O) operations.

In Unix-like systems, everything is a file. This means the device itself will be available by a device file (/dev/xxx). Thus, we first determine the device file to see how the USB drive is recognized by the system. To do so, we will use the fdisk utility. The fdisk tool is usually used to format drives. However, with the help of the -l parameter, it presents a list of all the attached drives and partitions. This way, we determine that the USB disk is recognized as /dev/sda. The SD card of the Banana Pi is /dev/mmcblk0.

On a lot of published Linux distributions for the Banana Pi, a service called udisks is preinstalled. This program enables the automounting of various external devices. Therefore, the chances are good that the USB disk is already mounted when plugging it in.

To check that, we use the mount command piped to the grep command. As we used the mount command without any parameters, a list of all the currently mounted devices is outputted. By piping the output to the grep command, we filter this list to only show lines containing the string sda. If we see a result, we know that the USB drive is already mounted by the system. If this is the case, we want to unmount the USB disk to manually mount it afterwards. Unmounting is done by the umount command (not unmount) followed by the path or device file to unmount.

To mount a drive, we have to use a target directory to mount the disk into. In our example, we are creating a new directory /media/usb_drive using the mkdir (make directory) command.

Then we mount the first partition (`/dev/sda1`) into that new directory. The `mount` command takes at least the device file and the target directory as parameters (in that order). We also use the `-o umask=000` parameter. This means that we add an option (`-o`) to give everybody on the system read/write permissions on that volume. This is necessary as otherwise, the USB disk will be readable and writeable by the root user only.

Finally, we show all contents of the USB disk by executing the `ls` (list directory contents) command. In combination with the parameter `-la`, we are outputting the contents as a detailed list (`-l`; one line per file and directory), and outputting all (`-a`) contents, including hidden directories and files.

There's more...

While USB drives are removable media, they should be mounted into directories under `/media`. On the other hand, you may mount drives that you do not remove often into directories under `/mnt`. However, this is just a recommendation. Technically, it does not matter whether you put your target directories under `/media` or `/mnt`.

While executing the mount command, we used the `mount` option `umask=000`. This way we overwrite the default behavior, which mounts the USB disk with the permissions of the current process. As mounting requires root permissions, the default permissions will imply root access to the mounted directory only.

Filesystem permissions is an important concept in Unix-like systems. As Unix-like systems are able to handle multiple users, it is necessary to prevent users from accessing certain files or directories that they should not have access to (for example, system configuration files or files from other users). The filesystem permission concept adds methods to assign access rights for users and/or groups on the filesystem.

If you list the contents of the home directory (using `ls -l ~`), you will see certain details. Also, the permissions are shown when using the `-l` parameter of the command `ls`. The first column shows the permissions on each directory, for example:

```
drwxr-xr-x 3 bananapi pi ... Arduino
```

The first character (that is `d`) stands for directory and indicates that in this example, Arduino is a directory. The next three characters show the permissions for the *owner* (`bananapi`) of that directory. The `rwx` permissions mean that the owner has the right to read (`r`), write (`w`), and execute (`x`) the directory. The next three characters show the rights for the group (`pi`). As for the owner, all the members of the group `pi` have the right to read and execute that directory, but are not allowed (`-`) to write to the directory. The same goes for the last three characters that are all others.

By using the `umask=000` options parameter when mounting the USB drive, we are removing the default rights, resulting in all permissions to the target directory being granted.

See also

▸ A lot of essential commands were mentioned in this recipe. It is encouraged to spend some time learning the commands `ls`, `mkdir`, `mount`, and `umount`. Also, the permission system is incredibly important and the cause of a lot of misunderstandings and possible errors.

▸ The Wikipedia article about the filesystem permissions at `https://en.wikipedia.org/wiki/File_system_permissions#Notation_of_traditional_Unix_permissions` explains the Unix-notation of filesystem permissions.

Mounting an SSD or HDD via SATA

Besides the mounting of disks via USB, the Banana Pi provides a SATA interface. This interface provides greatly improved performance compared to USBs for h**ard disk drives** (**HDD**) or **solid state disks** (**SSD**).

Getting ready

This recipe requires the following ingredients:

▸ A Banana Pi

▸ USB power supply unit

▸ An SD card containing a Linux distribution

▸ A hard disk drive or solid state drive

▸ A SATA-to-SATA cable and a SATA power supply for your drive or SATA cable with power supply terminals

▸ Access to the Banana Pi's shell

All these products can be bought from retailers. The SATA cable with power supply terminals is quite rare. You might search for that item on online stores that specialize in single-board computers. If you search for *Banana Pi SATA cable with power terminals* or similar on your desired search engine, you will find retailers for that product.

How to do it...

The mounting of an external drive via SATA is similar to the mounting of a USB flash drive we discovered in the previous recipe. The only difference is the attaching of the drive before powering on the Banana Pi.

1. Before powering on your Banana Pi, attach one end of the SATA cable to your external drive.

2. Attach the other end to your Banana Pi.

3. Attach the power supply for your SATA drive.

4. If you have a SATA cable that comes with power supply terminals, attach the terminals to your Banana Pi. The following picture shows a 2.5" HDD attached to the Banana Pi via this combination.

5. Power your Banana Pi and initiate the boot sequence.

6. Open a shell.

7. Determine the SATA drive using the `fdisk` command:

   ```
   $ sudo fdisk -l
   ```

8. Create a directory to mount the SATA disk into:

   ```
   $ sudo mkdir /mnt/sata_drive
   ```

9. Mount an NTFS or FAT32 partition of the SATA disk into that directory:

   ```
   $ sudo mount -o umask=000 /dev/sda1 /mnt/sata_drive
   ```

10. If you have a partition with a Linux filesystem (such as ext4), you cannot use the `umask` option; in this case, you have to omit this option:

    ```
    $ sudo mount /dev/sda1 /mnt/sata_drive
    ```

You have mounted your SATA disk successfully.

How it works...

Make sure that your external drive is supplied with a sufficient power source. The Banana Pi can supply 2.5" drives with enough power. However 3.5" drives usually require too much energy. Therefore, you have to use an external power supply if you want to attach a 3.5" HDD to your Banana Pi.

[When using the Banana Pi as a power supply for the HDD, make sure that your Banana Pi itself has enough energy. In this case, I recommend using at least a 2000mA (2A) USB power supply.]

The mounting itself works just like the mounting of a USB drive or any other disk using the `mount` command. Just as before, we need a destination directory, which we created earlier.

If you try mounting a partition containing a Linux filesystem, you cannot use the `umask` option. In contrast to FAT32 or NTFS, Linux filesystems fully support the Unix-permission concept. Therefore, you have to work with the standard tools `chmod`, `chown`, and `chgrp` to assign or revoke access rights.

Mounting via fstab

In this recipe, we are going to automount our drives using the `fstab` (located at `/etc/fstab`) system file.

Getting ready

The following components are required to mount drives conveniently using the `fstab` file:

  ▸ A working Linux system on the Banana Pi

  ▸ A USB flash drive and/or a SATA drive

  ▸ In case of a SATA drive, a working connection to your Banana Pi and a suitable power supply

  ▸ Access to the Banana Pi's shell

How to do it...

Perform the following to configure a drive in your `fstab`:

1. Connect your devices accordingly.

2. Power your Banana Pi and initiate the boot sequence.

3. Open a shell.

4. Determine the used filesystems by `blkid` on attached partitions:

```
$ sudo blkid
```

5. You will get information about all the available partitions. In the following screenshot, you see that the drive `/dev/sda` has three partitions (sda1 using ext4, sda2 using FAT32, and sda3 using NTFS):

```
bananapi@lemaker ~ $ sudo blkid
/dev/mmcblk0p1: SEC_TYPE="msdos" LABEL="boot" UUID="787C-2FD4" TYPE="vfat"
/dev/mmcblk0p2: UUID="3d81d9e2-7d1b-4015-8c2c-29ec0875f762" TYPE="ext4"
/dev/sda1: UUID="c4f56218-9353-4758-a5f9-1a2eac08130d" TYPE="ext4"
/dev/sda2: UUID="298E-093C" TYPE="vfat"
/dev/sda3: UUID="7C4F20B572AAB23E" TYPE="ntfs"
```

6. Create the necessary target directories to mount these partitions:

```
$ sudo mkdir /mnt/ext4_partition
$ sudo mkdir /mnt/fat_partition
$ sudo mkdir /mnt/ntfs_partition
```

7. Edit `/etc/fstab` using a text editor such as nano with root privileges:

```
$ sudo nano /etc/fstab
```

8. Press and hold the down the arrow key until you reach the end of the `/etc/fstab`.

9. We configure all three partitions by adding three new lines:

```
/dev/sda1 /mnt/ext4_partition ext4 defaults 0 2
/dev/sda2 /mnt/fat_partition  vfat defaults 0 0
/dev/sda3 /mnt/ntfs_partition ntfs defaults 0 0
```

The following screenshot shows the three added partition definitions in the `fstab` file using the nano editor:

10. Exit the nano editor and save the changes by pressing *Ctrl* + *X*, followed by *Y* and *Enter*.

You have configured your drive in the `fstab` file successfully. You can mount your partitions using, for example, `sudo mount /mnt/ntfs_partition` from now on. Furthermore, when rebooting your system, the partitions should be mounted automatically.

How it works...

You can automatically let your system mount your USB or SATA drives while booting. Linux systems use the `/etc/fstab` (filesystem table) configuration file to configure the drives to be mounted.

The `fstab` file can be used to define how disk partitions, other block devices, or remote filesystems should be mounted. It has a variety of possible configuration options. Each line in the `fstab` file represents mounting information for a partition or similar.

We add the information for our partitions by adding new lines to the `fstab` file. Each line in the `fstab` file consists of the following configuration parts separated by spaces:

- ▶ The mounted partition.
- ▶ The target directory.
- ▶ The filesystem type used by the partition.
- ▶ The mounting options.
- ▶ Dump flag, used by the dump utility to decide when to make a backup.
- ▶ Pass flag, used by the `fsck` (filesystem check) utility to decide in which order the filesystems have to be checked. Use either 0 (filesystem check disabled) or 2. The value 1 is reserved for the root filesystem.

There's more...

You can use either the device file as the first column, or a so-called unique identifier (UUID) of your partition. Using the `blkid` command, you see the UUIDs of the partitions (`c4f56218-9353-4758-a5f9-1a2eac08130d`, `298E-093C`, and `7C4F20B572AAB23E`). We could replace three of our lines in `fstab` with the following:

```
UUID=c4f56218-9353-4758-a5f9-1a2eac08130d /mnt/ext4_partition ext4
defaults 0 2
UUID=298E-093C /mnt/fat_partition vfat defaults 0 0
UUID=7C4F20B572AAB23E /mnt/ntfs_partition ntfs defaults 0 0
```

The advantage of this over the device file notation is that the kernel may use other device file nodes when rebooting with several devices attached. The UUID notation is unique and therefore safer.

Moreover, you can define specialized parameters for the mounting in the `mounting options` column of the `fstab` file. There are a lot of possible parameters. For example, if you want to mount a FAT32 partition and give everybody read/write access, you will use:

```
/dev/sda2 /mnt/fat_partition  vfat user,rw,umask=000 0 0
```

The FAT32 filesystem is supported by `vfat`. The `user` flag means that any user can mount the partition. Read/write access is permitted by the `rw` flag. The `umask=000` option removes selected rights.

See also

▸ The Wikipedia article about fstab configuration at `https://en.wikipedia.org/wiki/Fstab`

Booting from an external disk

This recipe explains how to copy the root filesystem from the SD card to an external disk and boot from it. This is an advanced recipe. You will still require an SD card as the kernel with the necessary filesystem drivers located at the first partition of the SD card.

You may want to move your root filesystem from the SD card to an external drive for performance and/or space reasons. Also when having a lot of I/O operations on the SD card, the SD card may become unstable. A filesystem on a SATA attached disk is more stable in general.

Getting ready

The following ingredients are needed when using an external disk as the root filesystem:

▸ A working Linux system on the Banana Pi

▸ A SATA HDD or SSD drive

▸ A working connection to your Banana Pi and a suitable power supply

▸ Access to the Banana Pi's shell

How to do it...

This recipe is split into two subtopics, the preparing (that is formatting) of the external disk and the copying and configuring of the root filesystem.

Formatting the drive

We need to prepare the HDD or SSD to have at least one formatted ext4 partition.

 In the following steps, we are *completely erasing* all the existing partitions on the hard drive to get one fresh ext4 partition. If you do not use a brand new drive, make a backup of its contents, as the drive will be wiped!

 If you have enough free space, you can also create a new ext4 partition without erasing the previous ones. In this case, you can use a tool like *gparted* for reducing a partition and creating another one.

1. Open a shell.
2. If your external drive is already mounted, unmount all partitions:

   ```
   $ sudo umount /dev/sda*
   ```

3. Execute the `fdisk` program with the SATA disk as parameter:

   ```
   $ sudo fdisk /dev/sda
   ```

4. When entering p, you get a list of all the currently available partitions.
5. We are going to delete all partitions.
6. Enter d followed by 1 to delete the first partition.
7. Use the d operation again, until all partitions are deleted.
8. Enter n followed by 4x. Press *Enter* to create a new partition with the full size of the drive.
9. Enter p again to check whether the partition table is correct.
10. Check again to see whether everything is correct. The next step is the point of no return.
11. Enter w to write the changes to the drive. Otherwise enter q to quit without changes.

    The following screenshot shows the previous steps done in `fdisk`:

```
bananapi@lemaker ~ $ sudo fdisk /dev/sda

The device presents a logical sector size that is smaller than
the physical sector size. Aligning to a physical sector (or optimal
I/O) size boundary is recommended, or performance may be impacted.

Command (m for help): p

Disk /dev/sda: 1000.2 GB, 1000204886016 bytes
255 heads, 63 sectors/track, 121601 cylinders, total 1953525168 sectors
Units = sectors of 1 * 512 = 512 bytes
Sector size (logical/physical): 512 bytes / 4096 bytes
I/O size (minimum/optimal): 4096 bytes / 4096 bytes
Disk identifier: 0x0005fd05

   Device Boot      Start         End      Blocks   Id  System
/dev/sda1            2048  1468008447   734003200    7  HPFS/NTFS/exFAT
/dev/sda2      1468008448  1953521663   242756608   83  Linux

Command (m for help): d
Partition number (1-4): 1

Command (m for help): d
Selected partition 2

Command (m for help): n
Partition type:
   p   primary (0 primary, 0 extended, 4 free)
   e   extended
Select (default p):
Using default response p
Partition number (1-4, default 1):
Using default value 1
First sector (2048-1953525167, default 2048):
Using default value 2048
Last sector, +sectors or +size{K,M,G} (2048-1953525167, default 1953525167):
Using default value 1953525167

Command (m for help): p

Disk /dev/sda: 1000.2 GB, 1000204886016 bytes
255 heads, 63 sectors/track, 121601 cylinders, total 1953525168 sectors
Units = sectors of 1 * 512 = 512 bytes
Sector size (logical/physical): 512 bytes / 4096 bytes
I/O size (minimum/optimal): 4096 bytes / 4096 bytes
Disk identifier: 0x0005fd05

   Device Boot      Start         End      Blocks   Id  System
/dev/sda1            2048  1953525167   976761560   83  Linux

Command (m for help): w
The partition table has been altered!

Calling ioctl() to re-read partition table.
Syncing disks.
```

12. Create the ext4 filesystem on the newly created partition:

    ```
    $ sudo mkfs.ext4 /dev/sda1
    ```

13. After a few seconds to minutes, the new ext4 partition is created.

You have created a fresh ext4 partition successfully.

Copying the root filesystem and editing uEnv.txt

The second step is to copy the whole root filesystem (rootfs) to the external disk and edit the `uEnv.txt` file, which contains essential information for the kernel at boot time:

1. Create two mount directories (if not existent) to mount the first partition of the SD card and the SATA drive:

    ```
    $ sudo mkdir /mnt/boot
    ```

    ```
    $ sudo mkdir /mnt/sata_drive
    ```

2. Mount the partitions of your SD card:

    ```
    $ sudo mount /dev/mmcblk0p1 /mnt/boot
    ```

3. Mount the new ext4 partition of your SATA drive:

    ```
    $ sudo mount /dev/sda1 /mnt/sata_drive
    ```

4. Synchronize the rootfs to the SATA drive:

    ```
    $ sudo rsync -arxP / /mnt/sata_drive/
    ```

5. You will see that all the files are synchronized from the root to the SATA drive. This will take some time.

6. As soon as the progress is done, edit the `uEnv.txt` to change the used root:

    ```
    $ sudo nano /mnt/boot/uEnv.txt
    ```

7. In the last line, you will find a configuration option `root=/dev/mmcblk0p2`. You might need to scroll to the right-hand side by pressing the right arrow key.

8. Edit this option to `root=/dev/sda1`:

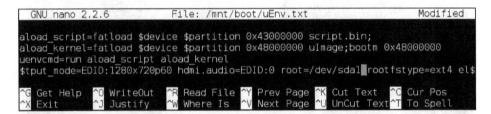

9. Exit and save nano by pressing *Ctrl + X*, followed by *Y* and *Enter*.

10. To verify that everything is written to the SD card, execute sync:

    ```
    $ sync
    ```

11. Reboot your Banana Pi from the external drive:

    ```
    $ sudo shutdown -r now
    ```

You successfully booted your Banana Pi from the external disk.

How it works...

The Linux kernel is located on the first partition of the SD card (filename `uImage`). When powering the Banana Pi, the boot loader (called UBoot) tries to load the kernel from the SD card. The kernel itself requires some parameters to boot successfully. These parameters and options are configured in the `uEnv.txt` file.

When writing the SD card to prepare a Linux distribution for the Banana Pi, the image contains two partitions. The first partition includes the kernel, the `uEnv.txt` and a `script.bin` files. The second partition is the actual root filesystem. The rootfs contains all the actual programs, configurations, home directories, and so on of your Linux system.

We are synchronizing the rootfs from the SD card to a partition on the external drive using the synchronization tool *rsync*. The tool rsync is used to synchronize files over a network or on two directories, as in this case. The parameters `-a` mean archive (preserving permissions, symbolic links, and so on), `-r` recursive (recursive into directories), and `-x` is to prevent crossing filesystem boundaries. The parameter `-P` shows the progress of each synchronization.

Then we change the desired root from the rootfs of the SD card (that is the second partition) to the partition of the external drive in the `uEnv.txt`.

As the boot loader requires the kernel and further information from the first partition of an SD card, the SD card cannot be omitted when moving the rootfs to an external drive.

To use the SD card again as root, you simply mount the first SD card again and change the root option back to `root=/dev/mmcblk0p2`.

See also

- A great yet simple guide on how to use fdisk—the How to Use Fdisk to Manage Partitions on Linux article at `http://www.howtogeek.com/106873/how-to-use-fdisk-to-manage-partitions-on-linux/`
- The manual page of rsync by its developers—the HTML version of the rsync man page at `https://download.samba.org/pub/rsync/rsync.html`

4
Networking

In this chapter, we will cover the following recipes:

- ▸ Sharing files over the network via Samba
- ▸ Setting up a web application
- ▸ Securing the Nginx web server using SSL
- ▸ Synchronizing files over the Internet
- ▸ Controlling the desktop remotely using VNC
- ▸ Securing SSH using SSH keys
- ▸ Setting up a UPnP media server

Introduction

This chapter will present the recipe for common networking tasks using the Banana Pi. One of the key strengths of the device is the fast network adapters that provide—especially combined with the SATA interface—the base of powerful network applications.

Sharing files over the network via Samba

This recipe will show how to set up a Samba server on the Banana Pi. Moreover, we will investigate how we can connect Windows and Linux clients to the Samba server. Samba is a re-implementation of the SMB/CIFS networking protocol to provide file and print sharing among Windows and Linux systems.

For this recipe, you require the following:

▸ A running Banana Pi with a Debian-based Linux system

▸ A configured network on the Banana Pi

How to do it...

We are splitting this recipe into the installation and configuration of the Samba server and the setup of clients.

Installing the Samba server

Installing the Samba server is done quickly.

We are working with the default user `bananapi` in the upcoming recipe. Furthermore, we are using the default hostname `lemaker`. If you have your own user or hostname, replace in the following steps where appropriate:

1. Open a shell.

2. Create a directory that is shared later:

    ```
    $ mkdir /home/bananapi/first_share
    ```

3. Put a test file into the future share:

    ```
    $ touch /home/bananapi/first_share/helloworld.txt
    ```

4. Install the server, common tools, and the client via `apt-get`:

    ```
    $ sudo apt-get install samba samba-common-bin samba-client
    ```

     Sometimes, it is necessary to update the Apt cache before you are able to install packages. This happens if your Apt cache is outdated and there is a newer package version available than listed in your Apt cache. If you get an error like `Failed to fetch ... 404 Not Found`, then you likely require an Apt cache update like `$ sudo apt-get update`.

5. Backup the default `/etc/samba/smb.conf`:

    ```
    $ sudo cp /etc/samba/smb.conf /etc/samba/smb.conf.backup
    ```

    If anything goes wrong in the following steps, you can always revert the default `smb.conf` by copying back `smb.conf.backup`.

6. Configure the server by editing `/etc/samba/smb.conf`:

   ```
   $ sudo nano /etc/samba/smb.conf
   ```

7. You will find a large file with a lot of comments (lines beginning with # that are ignored by the server).

8. Scroll down to the end using the down arrow key and add a `share` definition with the following configuration:

   ```
   [first_share]
     comment = My first share
     read only = no
     locking = no
     path = /home/bananapi/first_share
     guest ok = no
   ```

9. Save and exit the file by pressing *Ctrl + X*, followed by *Y* and *Enter*.

10. Now, we have to create a Samba user. In our case, we add a Samba user named `bananapi`:

    ```
    $ sudo smbpasswd -a bananapi
    ```

     Keep in mind that the Samba user must exist as a Linux user on your system. Add a Linux user with the same name as we have seen in *Chapter 2, Administration*, before adding a Samba user.

11. You will have to assign a password and retype it.

12. The `smbpasswd` tool will respond with `Added user bananapi`.

13. Restart the Samba server:

    ```
    $ sudo /etc/init.d/samba restart
    ```

     The restarting of a server application may differ depending on your operating system. For example, on Lubuntu, the correct command is:

    ```
    $ sudo service smbd restart
    ```

14. Test whether the share and server are recognized:

    ```
    $ smbclient -L localhost -U%
    ```

15. You should see information about your Samba server on the console. The following screenshot shows an example output:

```
bananapi@lemaker ~ $ smbclient -L localhost -U%
Domain=[WORKGROUP] OS=[Unix] Server=[Samba 3.6.6]

        Sharename       Type      Comment
        ---------       ----      -------
        print$          Disk      Printer Drivers
        first_share     Disk      My first share
        IPC$            IPC       IPC Service (lemaker server)
Domain=[WORKGROUP] OS=[Unix] Server=[Samba 3.6.6]

        Server          Comment
        ---------       -------
        LEMAKER         lemaker server

        Workgroup       Master
        ---------       -------
        WORKGROUP
```

16. Now, we test to see whether the share itself is accessible via the `bananapi` Samba user:

    `$ smbclient -U bananapi //localhost/first_share`

17. You should see the SMB command line. Type the `dir` command to get a list of files:

    `smb: \> dir`

18. If you see our previous created `helloworld.txt`, you have set up the Samba share successfully. The following screenshot shows the result:

```
bananapi@lemaker ~ $ smbclient -U bananapi //localhost/first_share
Enter bananapi's password:
Domain=[WORKGROUP] OS=[Unix] Server=[Samba 3.6.6]
smb: \> dir
  .                                   D        0  Mon Mar 16 17:54:18 2015
  ..                                  D        0  Mon Mar 16 17:14:06 2015
  helloworld.txt                               0  Mon Mar 16 17:54:18 2015

                48269 blocks of size 65536. 8510 blocks available
smb: \>
```

19. Quit the Samba command line using the `quit` command:

    `smb: \> quit`

You can now try to access the share from another computer.

Accessing the Samba share on Windows

Accessing the shared directory on Windows is simple. Perform the following on your Windows computer:

1. Open the Windows Explorer (for example, by pressing the Windows logo key + *E*).

2. Click onto the address bar (or press *Ctrl + L*).

3. Type the following URL into the address bar:

    `\\lemaker\first_share`

If your computer does not recognize the hostname `lemaker`, try to use the IP address of your Banana Pi instead.

4. You are requested to enter your Samba user credentials.

5. Type the username `bananapi` and the password `bananapi`.

6. If the login does not work, try to prefix the username: `lemaker\bananapi`.

7. You should be logged in successfully and see the test file we created:

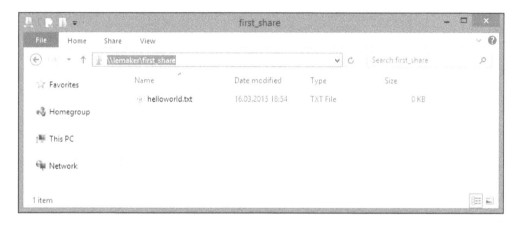

8. If you can access your share, you might also create a so-called network location. It enables you to work with your Samba share as if it was a local disk.

9. Open the Command Prompt (for example, by pressing Windows logo key + R and run the program `cmd.exe`).

10. Enter the following command to create a network location:

```
net use X: \\lemaker\first_share /P:Yes
```

11. As shown in this screenshot, the command will respond with: `The command completed successfully`:

12. Now you have a new network drive in your Windows Explorer with drive letter X:.

13. In the next screenshot, you can see the requested login credentials when accessing the network share. Click onto the **Remember my credentials** checkbox to log in automatically in the future.

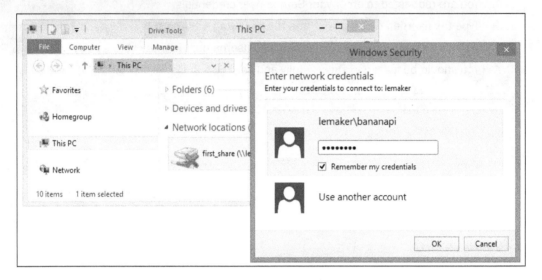

Accessing the Samba share on Linux manually

Also, on Linux, the accessing of the Samba share is quite simple. We can either mount the share manually using the command line or automatically using the `fstab` file. Either way, you must have the smbclient installed on your Linux computer.

1. Open a shell.

2. Create a target directory to mount the Samba share:

   ```
   $ sudo mkdir /mnt/samba_share
   ```

3. Mount the Samba share via the following command:

   ```
   $ sudo mount -t cifs //lemaker/first_share /mnt/samba_share/ -
   o user=bananapi,password=bananapi
   ```

 If your computer does not recognize the hostname `lemaker`, try to use the IP address of your Banana Pi instead.

As shown in the following screenshot, the Samba share is mounted successfully and can be accessed:

```
rel@gs70 ~ $ sudo mkdir /mnt/samba_share
[sudo] password for rel:
rel@gs70 ~ $ sudo mount -t cifs //lemaker/first_share /mnt/samba_share/ -o user=bananapi,password=bananapi
rel@gs70 ~ $ ls -la /mnt/samba_share
total 4
drwxr-xr-x 2 rel  1000     0 Mar 16 18:54 .
drwxr-xr-x 6 root root  4096 Mar 17 13:26 ..
-rw-r--r-- 1 rel  1000     0 Mar 16 18:54 helloworld.txt
```

Accessing the Samba share on Linux using fstab

To add the Samba share to your `fstab` and let it mount automatically, we do the following:

1. Open a shell.
2. Create the target directory if not existent:

   `$ sudo mkdir /mnt/samba_share`

3. Edit the `fstab` file with an editor such as nano:

   `$ sudo nano /etc/fstab`

4. Go to the end of the `fstab` file by pressing and holding the down arrow key.
5. Add the following line to `fstab`:

   ```
   //lemaker/first_share /mnt/samba_share cifs
   username=bananapi,password=bananapi 0 0
   ```

6. Exit and save nano by pressing *Ctrl + X*, followed by *Y* and *Enter*.
7. If the target directory `/mnt/samba_share` is already mounted, unmount it:

   `$ sudo umount /mnt/samba_share`

8. Now we mount the target directory by just entering the following command:

   `$ sudo mount /mnt/samba_share`

You should have access to the Samba share. Depending on your used Linux distribution, the share might be remounted automatically on boot or not. If it does not automount, consult your distributions manual for the appropriate automount configuration.

How it works...

As mentioned earlier, Samba is a so-called re-implementation of the SMB/CIFS protocol. These protocols are used by Windows to enable file and printer sharing over the local network. Therefore, installing a Samba server is a great choice if you have Windows and Linux computers on your local area network.

To create a so-called share, we previously needed a directory that is to be shared. In our case, it is the directory `/home/bananapi/first_share` on the Banana Pi. Of course, you are free to use any other directory as long as it has the correct permissions assigned. The using of a shared directory on an external disk is advisable as you usually have more space and a better performance compared to the SD card.

To test our share later on, we create a text file via the `touch` command. When executed without parameters, the `touch` command updates the access time of a file. If the file does not exist, a new text file is created. Just like in our case.

After installing the required Samba components, we have to configure the Samba server in order to make a directory accessible (to share it) over the network. The Samba server is configured by editing the system configuration file `/etc/samba/smb.conf`. In case the configuration fails for any reason, we backup the default `smb.conf` before we edit it.

We create a new share by adding a new section with the future name of the share (`[first_share]` in our example). The section itself contains the configuration options. There are several possible options that you can learn from the manual page of the Samba configuration (`$ man smb.conf`). For our purposes, it is suitable to configure our share like this:

- The share has a name/comment (`comment = My first share`)
- The share is readable and writable (`read only = no`)
- The share has locking disabled (`locking = no`)
- The share is accessible by Samba users only (`guest ok = no`)
- The directory that is to be shared (`path = /home/bananapi/first_share`)

As we configure our share to disallow anonymous guest logins, we need to create a Samba user. By using the `smbpasswd` command, we create a Samba user with the username and password `bananapi`.

When the previous configuration is finished, we have to restart the Samba server to apply the changes. On Debian-based distributions, most services are started and stopped using administrative shell scripts that are located under `/etc/init.d`.

When installing the Samba server, a script is provided under `/etc/init.d/samba` to control the Samba server. It is also run automatically on boot. We restart the Samba server by executing `/etc/init.d/samba` with the `restart` parameter. As mentioned earlier, the command may differ if you do not use the Raspbian operating system for your Banana Pi. Look up the manual of your operating system.

Later, we test to see whether we have access to the share locally on the Banana Pi. To do so, we execute the smbclient tool. The parameter `-L` lists information about a Samba host. The `-U%` parameter means that a username and password are not used, which results in obtaining anonymous server information. If we want to access the shared directory using smbclient, we have to use login credentials (as we have disallowed anonymous guests on that share). This is why we use `-U bananapi` in the second smbclient run, where you will be asked for a password.

As the SMB/CIFS protocol is widely used in the Windows world, we can conveniently access our share from a Windows client. To access the share, we are using the Windows notation with backslashes (\\hostname\share_name). If your computer cannot recognize the Banana Pi by its hostname, you have to use the IP address instead. Also, we can mount the share as a drive by executing the net program on the command line. Alternatively, you can also assign a network location by right-clicking on **This PC**, choosing **Add a network location** in Windows Explorer and following the configuration wizard.

On Linux clients, we have similar possibilities by using either the mount command or configuring a share in /etc/fstab. In both cases, the access will only work if we have the smbclient tool installed on our Linux client computer.

There's more...

Make sure that on the Samba server, the shared directory and its parent directories have read and executed permissions for all users (for example, the permissions drwxr-xr-x). You can add, read, and execute permissions for all users using the chmod command:

```
$ sudo chmod a+rx /home/bananapi/first_share
```

The chmod command (change file mode bits) assigns permissions for directories or files. The a+rx parameter means for *all* (a), *add* (+), *read* (r), and *execute* (x) permissions.

To list all Samba users on your Banana Pi, you can use the pdbedit tool:

```
$ sudo pdbedit -w -L
```

To delete a Samba user (not the actual Linux user), you can also use the smbpasswd command:

```
$ sudo smbpasswd -x bananapi
```

On Debian distributions, you generally have two controlling services (server applications or daemons). We mentioned the classic *System V* method by executing the shell script in /etc/init.d. You can also control daemons using the service program.

For example, the Samba daemon is also restarted by executing the following command:

```
$ sudo service samba restart
```

Also, the previous alternative may differ depending on your operating system. Technically, it does not matter which method you use in almost all cases. The service method uses System V scripts as well, but in a cleaner environment without potential issues caused by environmental variables or the like.

Another security concern about `fstab` on Linux clients is that normally every user can read the contents of the file `/etc/fstab` (it has `-rw-r--r--` permissions). Therefore, if you have more than one user on your system, the other users can easily read the contents of the `fstab` file, which includes the login data for the Samba share. Therefore, you are able to exclude the login credentials into another file, which is only readable by the root user. Then you just refer to that credentials file in `fstab`:

1. Open a shell.

2. Open nano to create a new credentials file:

   `$ sudo nano /etc/samba/bananapi.cred`

3. In the editor, add the following two lines:

   ```
   username=bananapi
   password=bananapi
   ```

4. Exit and save nano by pressing *Ctrl + X*, followed by *Y* and *Enter*.

5. Revoke all permissions for groups for our newly created file:

   `$ sudo chmod go-rwx /etc/samba/bananapi.cred`

6. From now on, the file is readable and writable for the root user only.

7. Edit the `fstab` file to refer to the credentials file:

   `$ sudo nano /etc/fstab`

8. Modify the line defining the mount-point for the share to:

   ```
   //lemaker/first_share /mnt/samba_share cifs
   credentials=/etc/samba/bananapi.cred 0 0
   ```

9. Exit and save nano by pressing *Ctrl + X*, followed by *Y* and *Enter*.

In this way, users can see that there is a credentials file used for the Samba share. However, as we revoked the reading permissions, apart from the root user, there is no way to read the actual username and password for that share. The chmod parameter `go-rwx` means for *group* (g) and *all others* (o), *revoke* (-) *reading* (r), *writing* (w) and *execute* (x) permissions.

See also

▶ The Wikipedia article about Samba at `https://en.wikipedia.org/wiki/Samba_(software)`

▶ SambaServerSimple on Debian wiki—a small guide on how to set up Samba —at `https://wiki.debian.org/SambaServerSimple`

▶ The manual page about `smb.conf`, using the following command:

   `man smb.conf`

- ▸ The manual page about `smbpasswd`, using the following command:

`man smbpasswd`

Setting up a web application

In this recipe, we are going to explore the possibilities of the Banana Pi to run dynamic web applications. We will install the Nginx web server, the MySQL database server, and the PHP scripting language. In order to get this complete, we are going to set up the widely used blog software, WordPress, on top of our upcoming web stack.

Getting ready

The following ingredients are required to cook the web stack:

- ▸ A running Banana Pi with a Debian-based Linux system
- ▸ A configured network on the Banana Pi

How to do it...

We need to split this recipe into four parts.

- ▸ The setup of the web server
- ▸ The setup of the database server
- ▸ The setup of PHP
- ▸ The setup of WordPress

Installing the Nginx web server

There are a number of web servers on the market. In this recipe, we are going to use the Nginx (pronounced *engine-x*) web server as it performs well with the Banana Pi.

To set up the Nginx software, perform the following:

1. Open a shell.
2. Install Nginx:

```
$ sudo apt-get install nginx
```

3. Apt will ask you to confirm the installation of dependency packages.
4. Enter Y to confirm the dependency packages and continue the installation. After a few seconds to minutes, the web server is installed.

5. The next step is to configure Nginx. Edit `/etc/nginx/sites-available/default`:

   `$ sudo nano /etc/nginx/sites-available/default`

6. Scroll down until you see the first server section (`server {`).

7. You will see the so-called HTTP root (`root /usr/share/nginx/www`). In this directory, we are going to put our files.

> Depending on your operating system, the HTTP root may also differ. For example, on Lubuntu, the HTTP root directory is `/usr/share/nginx/html`. Keep this in mind for the next steps and recipes.

8. Below the `root` entry, you see an `index` entry. Add `index.php` to the index list, so that the line looks like this:

   `index index.html index.htm index.php;`

9. Scroll down again until you reach the commented out PHP section (`#location ~ \.php$ {`).

10. Uncomment the whole section except for the line: `fastcgi_pass 127.0.0.1:9000`.

11. Your configuration file should look similar to the one shown in the next screenshot:

```
  GNU nano 2.2.6      File: /etc/nginx/sites-available/default      Modified

        #
        location ~ \.php$ {
                fastcgi_split_path_info ^(.+\.php)(/.+)$;
                # NOTE: You should have "cgi.fix_pathinfo = 0;" in php.ini

                # With php5-cgi alone:
        #       fastcgi_pass 127.0.0.1:9000;
                # With php5-fpm:
                fastcgi_pass unix:/var/run/php5-fpm.sock;
                fastcgi_index index.php;
                include fastcgi_params;
        }

        # deny access to .htaccess files, if Apache's document root
        # concurs with nginx's one
        #
        #location ~ /\.ht {
        #       deny all;

^G Get Help  ^O WriteOut   ^R Read File  ^Y Prev Page  ^K Cut Text   ^C Cur Pos
^X Exit      ^J Justify    ^W Where Is   ^V Next Page  ^U UnCut Text ^T To Spell
```

12. Exit and save the nano editor by pressing *Ctrl + X*, followed by *Y* and *Enter*.

13. Restart the Nginx web server to apply the changes:

    `$ sudo /etc/init.d/nginx restart`

We have just installed the Nginx web server and prepared it to run PHP applications. You can check whether your web server is running. Enter the URL `http://HOSTNAME/` (for example, `http://lemaker/`) into a browser that is on the same network. As mentioned in the previous recipes, you can also use the IP address of your Banana Pi instead of the hostname. You should see a page similar to the following screenshot:

Installing the PHP scripting language

The next step is to install the PHP interpreter for our Nginx web server.

1. With the shell opened, install the following packages:

    ```
    $ sudo apt-get install php5-fpm php5-mysql
    ```

2. Apt will ask you to confirm the installation of the dependency packages.

3. Enter Y to continue the installation.

4. Apt will configure some files. This may take a few minutes.

5. After installing PHP, we are going to change the permissions of the HTTP root, so that our user can place files into that directory flawlessly:

    ```
    $ sudo chown -R $USER.$GROUP /usr/share/nginx/www
    ```

    > Replace the HTTP root directory with the correct HTTP root depending on your operating system.

6. Then we create a PHP script to test the PHP functionality with Nginx:

    ```
    $ nano /usr/share/nginx/www/info.php
    ```

7. In the nano editor, we write the following PHP code:

    ```
    <?php
    phpinfo();
    ```

8. Exit and save the newly created file by pressing *Ctrl + X*, followed by *Y* and *Enter*.

Now, PHP should be installed correctly. We test it by opening a browser and using the URL `http://lemaker/info.php`.

You should see a page with a lot of information about your PHP setup, as shown in the next screenshot:

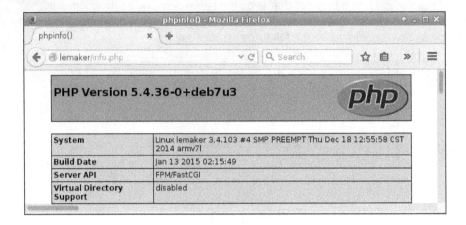

Installing the MySQL database server

Now that the web server is running and serving dynamic PHP pages, we need to install a database server as a lot of web applications require a database server:

1. With the shell open, install the MySQL server:

   ```
   $ sudo apt-get install mysql-server
   ```

2. Apt will ask you to confirm the installation of dependency packages.

3. Enter Y to continue the installation.

4. After some seconds, you will see a **Package configuration** wizard with a blue background on your shell.

5. Choose a password for your MySQL root user. We are using bananapi.

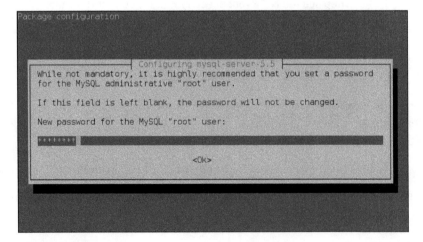

6. Repeat the chosen password as requested in the next step.

7. Apt will continue configuring the MySQL server.

8. We install the default MySQL system tables:

   ```
   $ sudo mysql_install_db
   ```

9. Then we secure our setup:

   ```
   $ sudo /usr/bin/mysql_secure_installation
   ```

10. Enter your chosen MySQL root password when prompted.

11. You can change your password here, but we continue without changing the root password by entering n.

12. When requested whether to remove anonymous users, enter Y.

13. Disallow the remote login of the root by entering Y in the next step.

14. Next, we remove the test databases by entering Y.

15. Finally, we reload the privileges by entering Y.

We have MySQL installed successfully and can continue installing the blogging software WordPress.

Installing WordPress

WordPress is an open source blogging web application and content management system (CMS). It is programmed in PHP and uses MySQL as a database backend. In this section, we are going to install WordPress and create a test post:

1. With a shell open, download the latest WordPress archive into the HTTP root of Nginx:

   ```
   $ cd /usr/share/nginx/www
   $ wget http://wordpress.org/latest.tar.gz
   ```

   This will download WordPress blogging software.

2. When the download is finished, we unpack the downloaded archive:

   ```
   $ tar -xzvf latest.tar.gz
   ```

3. We have to create a new MySQL database for our WordPress setup. Enter the command-line tool for MySQL:

   ```
   $ mysql -u root -p
   ```

4. Enter the MySQL root password.

5. Add the new database in the MySQL command-line tool:

   ```
   mysql> CREATE DATABASE wordpress;
   ```

6. Then we create a MySQL user and allow access to the new database:

```
mysql> GRANT ALL PRIVILEGES ON wordpress.* TO
wordpress@localhost IDENTIFIED BY "wordpress_password";
```

7. Reload the privileges to apply the changes:

```
mysql> FLUSH PRIVILEGES;
```

8. Quit the MySQL command line:

```
mysql> EXIT
```

```
bananapi@lemaker /usr/share/nginx/www $ mysql -u root -p
Enter password:
Welcome to the MySQL monitor.  Commands end with ; or \g.
Your MySQL connection id is 50
Server version: 5.5.41-0+wheezy1 (Debian)

Copyright (c) 2000, 2014, Oracle and/or its affiliates. All rights reserved.

Oracle is a registered trademark of Oracle Corporation and/or its
affiliates. Other names may be trademarks of their respective
owners.

Type 'help;' or '\h' for help. Type '\c' to clear the current input statement.

mysql> CREATE DATABASE wordpress;
Query OK, 1 row affected (0.00 sec)

mysql> GRANT ALL PRIVILEGES ON wordpress.* TO wordpress@localhost IDENTIFIED BY
"wordpress_password";
Query OK, 0 rows affected (0.00 sec)

mysql> FLUSH PRIVILEGES;
Query OK, 0 rows affected (0.00 sec)

mysql> EXIT
Bye
bananapi@lemaker /usr/share/nginx/www $
```

9. As shown in the preceding screenshot, the MySQL command line will respond with `Bye`.

10. After setting up our WordPress database, we have to configure the database information for WordPress. Rename `wp-config-sample.php` to `wp-config.php`:

```
$ cd /usr/share/nginx/www/wordpress

$ mv wp-config-sample.php wp-config.php
```

11. Edit the `wp-config.php` file:

```
$ nano wp-config.php
```

12. Within the `wp-config.php` file, scroll down to the define functions.

13. Modify the define values to the following:

```
define('DB_NAME', 'wordpress');
define('DB_USER', 'wordpress');
define('DB_PASSWORD', 'wordpress_password');
```

14. Your `wp-config.php` file should look like as shown in the following screenshot.

```
  GNU nano 2.2.6              File: wp-config.php              Modified

// ** MySQL settings - You can get this info from your web host ** //
/** The name of the database for WordPress */
define('DB_NAME', 'wordpress');

/** MySQL database username */
define('DB_USER', 'wordpress');

/** MySQL database password */
define('DB_PASSWORD', 'wordpress_password');

/** MySQL hostname */
define('DB_HOST', 'localhost');

/** Database Charset to use in creating database tables. */
define('DB_CHARSET', 'utf8');

/** The Database Collate type. Don't change this if in doubt. */
define('DB_COLLATE', '');

/**#@+
 * Authentication Unique Keys and Salts.
 *
 * Change these to different unique phrases!
 * You can generate these using the {@link https://api.wordpress.org/secret-key$
 * You can change these at any point in time to invalidate all existing cookies$
 *
 * @since 2.6.0

^G Get Help  ^O WriteOut  ^R Read File  ^Y Prev Page  ^K Cut Text  ^C Cur Pos
^X Exit      ^J Justify   ^W Where Is   ^V Next Page  ^U UnCut Text^T To Spell
```

15. Exit and save nano by pressing *Ctrl + X*, followed by *Y* and *Enter*.

16. Execute the setup script on your browser. Go to `http://lemaker/wordpress/wp-admin/install.php`.

17. Enter your desired login details into the installation form. We are using:

    ❑ Username: `bananapi_user`

    ❑ Password: `bananapi`

18. Click on **Install WordPress**.

19. The setup script will inform you that the installation was successful. The next screenshot shows the page that is shown after the successful installation:

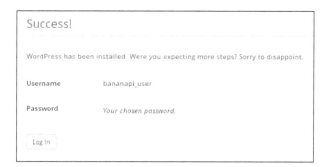

20. Click on **Log In**.

21. You will see the login mask of the WordPress administration page.

22. Enter your previously chosen login data (`bananapi_user` / `bananapi`).

23. You are logged into the administration page of WordPress.

24. Create a new blog post by clicking on **Posts** on the left menu and **Add New** on the upcoming page.

25. Enter a title and a blog post text, for example, refer to the following screenshot:

26. When finished, click on **Publish**.

27. To read your blog, open another browser tab and go to `http://lemaker/wordpress`.

Congratulations! You just have installed a blog application onto your Banana Pi. In the next screenshot, we see our previously created first blog post:

How it works...

Setting up a real web application such as WordPress from scratch is not a simple task. We have to install and configure several applications and the web application itself on top. But you are finished; you deployed a powerful web stack on your Banana Pi.

To run web applications in general, we must have a web server, a database server, a way to run scripting languages, and the desired web application. These components were installed in this recipe. Besides the installation, all components require configuration.

We started by configuring the default configuration of our web server Nginx. Within `/etc/nginx/sites-available/default`, we prepared the PHP support. Furthermore, we determined what the HTTP root directory is. It defines the directory that is used by Nginx to serve the websites. Open the browser and go to the hostname of the Banana Pi, the Nginx ascertains, if there is a so-called index file within the configured HTTP root directory and serves it. The index file is the *start page*. Indeed there is an `index.html` file within the HTTP root directory that contains HTML code.

This HTML is what Nginx sends to your browser, when going to `http://lemaker/`. The browser interprets the HTML code and you will see the message **Welcome to nginx!**.

A scripting language interpreter such as PHP enables us to run a program (a script) and let it create the HTML dynamically before the web server sends the HTML to the client. This is what happens when we create our `info.php` file containing just one PHP function: `phpinfo()`.

When using PHP code, we have to tell the PHP interpreter that the upcoming code should be interpreted. This is why we are beginning the `info.php` file with the PHP tag:

```
<?php
```

You can also end the PHP part by adding the closing tag `?>` at the end of the file. Still it is not necessary if the file is pure PHP (as in our example). Quite the contrary, it is preferable to omit the closing tag in pure PHP files.

So, when browsing the `info.php` file, the web server recognizes that we are requesting a page with a PHP script. Nginx then communicates with the **PHP-FPM** (**PHP FastCGI Process Manager**) service, which interprets the `info.php` file. The `phpinfo()` PHP function instructs the PHP interpreter to render information about the current PHP configuration as HTML. After the PHP interpreter finishes interpreting the PHP file, the produced HTML is sent back to Nginx. Nginx again serves the HTML from PHP via the HTTP protocol to the requesting browser.

If a lot of information needs to be saved for longer than one session, this information must be stored somehow. Sometimes data is stored in simple text files, but mostly they are stored in specialized databases. Most web applications store their data in databases. For example, the blog posts or user information of our WordPress setup are stored in our created WordPress database. PHP is able to use various database servers as persistence backends.

We downloaded WordPress by using the command-line tool wget (full name is GNU Wget). It is a program that retrieves files from web servers similar to a browser without the output in a browser window. Therefore, it is a great tool to download files from the Internet using your shell.

Each web application should have its own database. All databases are maintained by a **DBMS** (**Database Management System**). We use the open source DBMS MySQL. DBMS has its own users and permissions system. Therefore, we use the MySQL command-line tool to create a WordPress database and a database user that has access to the WordPress database via a password.

These three components (database name, database user, and the password) need to be configured in the web application as well. As we use WordPress, these values are configured in the `wp-config.php` (WordPress configuration) file.

First, we need to rename the sample configuration by using the `mv` (move) command. The `mv` command can move files or directories to other directories. Be careful when using `mv`; you can easily overwrite files when moving a filename to a filename that already exists. Instead of renaming the sample file, you can also copy the sample file to a real configuration file:

```
$ cp wp-config-sample.php wp-config.php
```

After we have configured the database information in the `wp-config.php`, we can finish the setup by executing the `install.php` file. That is done using the browser. You will have to enter some information about your blog and create an administrator user for your blog. When the installation is finished, you can log in to the administrator backend of WordPress (`wp-admin`) and create your first blog post.

There's more...

You don't need to set up your MySQL database through the MySQL command line. There are more user-friendly tools. For example, one convenient tool is a web application itself called PhpMyAdmin.

Setting up PhpMyAdmin

You can set up PhpMyAdmin easily:

1. With your shell open, change the directory to your HTTP root:

   ```
   $ cd /usr/share/nginx/www/
   ```

2. Download the PhpMyAdmin archive:

   ```
   $ wget http://sourceforge.net/projects
   /phpmyadmin/files/latest/download -O phpmyadmin.zip
   ```

3. Unpack PhpMyAdmin:

   ```
   $ unzip phpmyadmin.zip
   ```

4. Optionally, rename the PhpMyAdmin folder that we created:

   ```
   $ mv phpMyAdmin* phpmyadmin
   ```

5. Change into the `phpmyadmin` directory:

   ```
   $ cd phpmyadmin
   ```

6. With your browser, go to `http://lemaker/phpmyadmin/`.

7. Log in with your MySQL root user credentials:

   ❑ Username: `root`

   ❑ Password: `bananapi`

You are now able to create and modify databases and tables via your web browser and will not need to configure databases on the command line anymore. However, for readability, we still use the MySQL command-line tool to create database.

The following screenshot shows the PhpMyAdmin interface after a successful login. On the left-hand side menu, you can see the WordPress database we created:

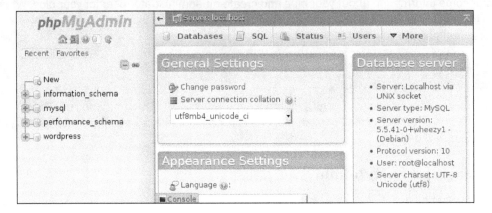

Other technologies

For performance and convenience reasons, we installed a web application stack based on Nginx, MySQL, and PHP. This is often called a LEMP stack (Linux, Engine-X, MySQL, and PHP). There are other possible stack configurations.

An even more often used web stack is based on the well-known Apache web server (the LAMP web stack). There are also other relational database servers such as PostgreSQL, the MySQL drop-in replacement MariaDB, and many more. Some PHP-based web applications require additional PHP modules that you may need to install through Apt. Furthermore, there exist alternative scripting languages such as JavaScript, Perl, Python, and Ruby that are widely used for web applications. Every technology has its own purpose and fills its own books.

However, our installed stack is suitable for a huge number of web applications as most web applications these days are using PHP and MySQL as its main backend technologies. Still you will need to check out the system requirements of your desired web application. For every technology, there are thousands of websites and books available on how to install and configure them.

In general, you will always need a web server, a database, and a scripting language interpreter for your web application. As you have mastered the basic concepts in this recipe, you will be able to set up almost any web application. Nearly all web applications have a website with an installation manual. It is recommended to follow these guidelines. Besides the system requirements and helpful tips that are mentioned, you will get to know your web application by following these installation manuals.

See also

▸ The official wiki from the developers of Nginx at `http://wiki.nginx.org`

▸ The official website of the PHP: Hypertext Preprocessor at `http://php.net/`

▸ A great online book about setting up and using MySQL at
`https://en.wikibooks.org/wiki/MySQL`

Securing the Nginx web server using SSL

As you may also want to access the Banana Pi from the Internet, you should think about the security aspect. In the previous recipe, we browsed our web applications via the default HTTP protocol. HTTP is not encrypted and is therefore vulnerable to various attacks. In this recipe, we are going to create a so-called SSL certificate to enable the encrypted **HTTPS** (**HTTP over SSL**) protocol.

Getting ready

The following ingredients are required to enable HTTPS on our Nginx web server:

▸ A running Banana Pi with a Debian-based Linux system

▸ A configured network on the Banana Pi

▸ A working Nginx web server as illustrated in the *Setting up a web application* recipe

How to do it...

We need to create an SSL certificate and add an HTTPS configuration to our Nginx web server.

Creating the certificate

We are going to create a self-signed certificate. In this recipe, we are using the hostname `lemaker`.

1. Open a shell.

2. Switch to `/etc/ssl`.

   ```
   $ cd /etc/ssl
   ```

3. Obtain a root shell:

   ```
   $ sudo -s
   ```

4. Create a private RSA key using the openssl application:

    ```
    # openssl genrsa 2048 > lemaker.key
    ```

    The RSA key generation will take a few seconds.

5. Create the certificate that is valid for 10 years:

    ```
    # openssl req -new -x509 -nodes -sha1 -days 3650 -key
    lemaker.key > lemaker.crt
    ```

6. You will be requested to enter some details about your certificate. Once the **Common Name** prompt appears, use `lemaker`:

7. Self-sign the certificate:

    ```
    # openssl x509 -noout -fingerprint -text < lemaker.crt >
    lemaker.info
    ```

8. Set read-only permissions for the root user to secure your private key:

    ```
    # chmod 400 lemaker.key
    ```

    The whole procedure is shown in the following screenshot:

```
bananapi@lemaker /etc/ssl $ sudo -s
[sudo] password for bananapi:
root@lemaker:/etc/ssl# openssl genrsa 2048 > lemaker.key
Generating RSA private key, 2048 bit long modulus
..........+++
......................+++
e is 65537 (0x10001)
root@lemaker:/etc/ssl# openssl req -new -x509 -nodes -sha1 -days 3650 -key lemak
er.key > lemaker.crt
You are about to be asked to enter information that will be incorporated
into your certificate request.
What you are about to enter is what is called a Distinguished Name or a DN.
There are quite a few fields but you can leave some blank
For some fields there will be a default value,
If you enter '.', the field will be left blank.
-----
Country Name (2 letter code) [AU]:US
State or Province Name (full name) [Some-State]:CA
Locality Name (eg, city) []:LA
Organization Name (eg, company) [Internet Widgits Pty Ltd]:Banana Pi
Organizational Unit Name (eg, section) []:Banana Pi
Common Name (e.g. server FQDN or YOUR name) []:lemaker
Email Address []:
root@lemaker:/etc/ssl# openssl x509 -noout -fingerprint -text < lemaker.crt > le
maker.info
root@lemaker:/etc/ssl# chmod 400 lemaker.key
root@lemaker:/etc/ssl# exit
bananapi@lemaker /etc/ssl $
```

9. Exit the root shell by pressing *Ctrl + D* or using the `exit` command.

We have now generated an SSL certificate. The next step is to configure Nginx to use that SSL certificate for HTTPS encryption.

Configuring Nginx to use an SSL certificate

Configuring Nginx to enable HTTPS is also done in `/etc/nginx/sites-available/default`. Let's see how this is done:

1. Within the opened shell, edit `/etc/nginx/sites-available/default`:

    ```
    $ sudo nano /etc/nginx/sites-available/default
    ```

2. In the server section, add the following configuration above the HTTP root configuration:

    ```
    listen 80;
    listen 443 ssl;
    ssl_certificate /etc/ssl/lemaker.crt;
    ssl_certificate_key /etc/ssl/lemaker.key;
    ```

    The specific part of your Nginx configuration should look like the next screenshot:

    ```
    GNU nano 2.2.6       File: /etc/nginx/sites-available/default

    server {
            #listen   80; ## listen for ipv4; this line is default
            #listen   [::]:80 default_server ipv6only=on; ## lister

            listen 80;
            listen 443 ssl;
            ssl_certificate      /etc/ssl/lemaker.crt;
            ssl_certificate_key /etc/ssl/lemaker.key;

            root /usr/share/nginx/www;
            index index.html index.htm index.php;
    ```

3. Exit and save nano by pressing *Ctrl + X*, followed by *Y* and *Enter*.

4. Restart the Nginx web server:

    ```
    $ sudo /etc/init.d/nginx restart
    ```

5. With your web browser, go to the HTTPS URL `https://lemaker/`.

6. You will see a warning on your browser **There is a problem with this websites's security certificate or This connection is Untrusted**.

7. Trust the connection in your browser:

    ❑ In Internet Explorer, click on **Continue** to this website (not recommended).

    ❑ In Firefox, click on **I understand the Risks** followed by **Add Exception**. In the upcoming window, click on **Confirm Security Exception**.

    ❑ In Chrome, click on **Advanced** followed by **Proceed to lemaker** (unsafe).

Your connection is now secured by HTTPS.

How it works...

The HTTPS protocol adds an encryption layer to the standard HTTP protocol. To do so, a *public key* and a *private key* is required. These keys are generated using the openssl application. The public key is integrated into the certificate we generated. The certificate is sent to the client, once he tries to connect to our web server via HTTPS. The browser checks the certificate and displays a warning. The warning occurs, because our certificate is not signed by a **Certificate Authority** (**CA**), but we self-signed it. The consequence is that your browser does not know the signer of our certificate (that is us) and displays the warning. Signing by a CA is costly in most cases. However, for our purposes, we do not need a CA-signed certificate.

So, once you have trusted our self-signed certificate, the communication with the server will be encrypted. It is recommended to use HTTPS for pages that require login credentials or other sensitive information (such as in WordPress or PhpMyAdmin).

To enable HTTPS support, we had to modify the Nginx configuration. In this recipe, we used two listen options in the configuration. One for port 80 (normal HTTP) and one for port 443 (HTTP over SSL). This means you can browse your Banana Pi via HTTP and HTTPS. If you want to disable HTTP at all, you can remove or comment out the `listen 80` line.

There's more...

The Mozilla Firefox browser handles certificates on its own. After confirming the security exception, you will not see the security warning anymore. However, other browsers or applications such as Internet Explorer or Chrome might handle the certificates differently. To avoid the warnings, you have to import the self-signed certificate into a certificate manager. This way, you trust your certificate and will not be interrupted by the browser warning any more.

Importing a self-signed certificate on Windows

We are going to import the certificate on Windows via Internet Explorer, but you are free to use whichever browser you want:

1. Open Internet Explorer.
2. Browse to `https://lemaker/`.
3. You will see the certificate warning in your browser.
4. Click on **Continue to this website** (not recommended) to trust the connection.
5. When you see the **Welcome to nginx!** message, click on the certificate error in the URL address bar above.
6. Click on **View Certificates**.
7. You will see a new **Certificate** window with information about our certificate.
8. Click on **Install Certificate...**

9. Select **Current User** to import the certificate for the current user only or **Local Machine** to import the certificate for everybody on the computer.

10. Click on **Next**.

11. Choose **Place all certificates in the following store** and click on **Browse**.

12. In the upcoming **Select Certificate Store** window, select **Trusted Root Certification Authorities**.

13. Close the window, by clicking on **OK**.

14. Click on **Next**, followed by **Finish**. You will see a final security warning.

15. Install the certificate by clicking on **Yes**. You will see a message **The import was successful**.

16. Click on **OK** on the message window and the certificate window to close both.

Your certificate is now imported as a root certificate. You will not see warning messages in the future. Keep in mind that the installation of the certificate is only valid for the common name we chose in the certificate generation. If you connect from the Internet to your Banana Pi using a Dynamic DNS service, you will have to issue a certificate for your DNS name.

Importing a self-signed certificate on Linux

Unfortunately, on Linux operating systems, there are several ways to import a certificate depending on your distribution and used application. Therefore, the following steps will not work on all distributions available, but at least Debian-based distributions:

1. Open a shell.

2. Install the `ca-certificates` and `gnutls-bin` package:

    ```
    $ sudo apt-get install ca-certificates gnutls-bin
    ```

3. Download the certificate information:

    ```
    $ gnutls-cli --print-cert lemaker < /dev/null >
    lemaker.crt.info
    ```

4. Extract only the certificate itself from the information:

    ```
    $ sed -ne '/-BEGIN CERTIFICATE-/,/-END CERTIFICATE-/p'
    lemaker.crt.info > lemaker.crt
    ```

5. Copy the certificate to the certificate store:

    ```
    $ sudo cp lemaker.crt /usr/local/share/ca-certificates/
    ```

6. Update the certificate store:

    ```
    $ sudo update-ca-certificates
    ```

7. To import a certificate for the Chromium browser, install `libnss3-tools` at first:

```
$ sudo apt-get install libnss3-tools
```

8. Then, add the certificate using `certutil`:

```
$ certutil -d sql:$HOME/.pki/nssdb -A -t "P,," -n lemaker -i
lemaker.crt
```

You have imported the certificate for most Linux applications and the Chromium browser.

See also

▶ The Wikipedia article about HTTPS at `https://en.wikipedia.org/wiki/HTTPS`

▶ A detailed guide on how to set up HTTPS on Nginx at `http://nginx.org/en/docs/http/configuring_https_servers.html`

Synchronizing files over the Internet

The Banana Pi is a great device for network applications. One especially interesting application is the synchronization of files over the Internet. In this recipe, we are going to set up the cloud solution ownCloud. ownCloud is an open source alternative to proprietary cloud solutions such as Dropbox, Google Drive, or Microsoft OneDrive. Once you have set up ownCloud, you can synchronize your data over the Internet and keep your data under your private control.

Getting ready

To set up an ownCloud solution, these ingredients are needed:

▶ A running Banana Pi with a Debian-based Linux system

▶ A configured network on the Banana Pi

▶ A working Nginx web server as illustrated in the *Setting up a web application* recipe

▶ A configured SSL certificate for your Nginx as explained in the *Securing the Nginx web server using SSL* recipe

How to do it...

To achieve synchronization over the Internet, you have to use a **Dynamic DNS** (**DDNS**) service to resolve your IP address to a domain. Later, we need to download and install ownCloud. Also, some configuration within Nginx needs to be done. Last but not least, we need to forward a port in our router settings.

Setting up a Dynamic DNS

This part is not really Banana Pi related, but is still required to access our Banana Pi from the Internet. There are several DDNS services available. We are going to use the `yDNS.eu` service as it is free and easy to use. However, you can use any DDNS service.

1. On your computer, browse to `https://ydns.eu/`.

2. Click on **Sign up** now.

3. Submit the upcoming form by entering your e-mail address, a desired password twice, and the requested captcha challenge.

4. After some minutes, you will receive an e-mail, including an activation link. Click on that activation link.

5. Click on **Sign in**.

6. Log in by entering your previously entered login details.

7. After you have logged in, click on **Create Host**.

8. Enter your desired hostname and select a domain. We will use `bananapi.ydns.eu`.

   The following screenshot shows the procedure to create a host on yDNS. You will need to use a different hostname, as `bananapi.ydns.eu` is already taken.

9. Click on **Create Host**.

10. You will see a list of all your created hosts, which is currently only one.

11. Your DDNS domain is set up correctly. Now, you can log out by clicking on your e-mail address on the upper-right corner followed by signing out.

The account creation for your Dynamic DNS hostname is done.

Updating the Dynamic DNS hostname

The next step is to let our Banana Pi automatically update the IP address of our DDNS domain periodically. To achieve this, we will create a shell script that updates the IP address on yDNS and is executed every 15 minutes via a cron job.

1. Open a shell on your Banana Pi.

2. Create a new directory for bash scripts and add a script with an editor like nano:

   ```
   $ mkdir /home/bananapi/scripts
   $ nano /home/bananapi/scripts/ydns_update.sh
   ```

3. Write the following bash script:

   ```
   #!/bin/bash
   USER=my_email@my_provider.com
   PASS=bananapi
   HOST=bananapi.ydns.eu
   curl --user $USER:$PASS https://ydns.eu/api/v1/update/?host=$HOST
   ```

   The following screenshot shows the bash script in the nano editor. Change the shell variables USER, PASS, and HOST according to your yDNS account and hostname details.

4. Exit and save nano by pressing *Ctrl + X*, followed by *Y* and *Enter*.

5. Make the created bash script executable:

   ```
   $ chmod a+x ~/scripts/ydns_update.sh
   ```

6. Test the script by executing it:

   ```
   $ /home/bananapi/scripts/ydns_update.sh
   ```

7. If your script responds with ok, your script is working correctly.

8. Now we set up a cron job to trigger that script every 15 minutes:

   ```
   $ crontab -e
   ```

9. Nano will be opened again but this time with the so-called crontab.

10. Scroll down to the last line and add:

    ```
    */15 * * * * /home/bananapi/scripts/ydns_update.sh
    ```

11. Exit and save nano by pressing *Ctrl + X*, followed by *Y* and *Enter*.

12. The cron job is installed now and will execute our update script every 15 minutes.

13. Test the DDNS domain using the `ping` command:

    $ ping bananapi.ydns.eu

    If ping shows the public IP address of your router, you have configured yDNS successfully.

14. Abort the ping program by pressing *Ctrl + C*.

Once we have created the DDNS domain and set up a cron job to update the domain regularly, we can move on by setting up a port forwarding to our Banana Pi.

Setting up a port forwarding

To enable a connection from the Internet to your Banana Pi, you usually need to open a port in your DSL or cable router. This mechanism is called **port forwarding**. Unfortunately, there are thousands of different routers on the market with different configuration interfaces. Therefore, it is impossible to explain the port forwarding for every router out there. Read the manual of your router on how to set up port forwarding. The following steps are valid if you use a Fritz!Box router by the manufacturer AVM. A good guide on how to set up a port forwarding for most routers on the market is found at `http://portforward.com`.

1. With your browser, go to your Fritz!Box configuration `http://fritz.box`.

2. Log in with your router administrator credentials.

3. Click on **Internet** on the right menu.

4. Click on the **Permit Access** in the **Internet** menu, followed by a click on the **Port Forwarding** tab.

5. Click on **New Port Forwarding**.

    We will set up a port forwarding for the HTTPS port (port 443) to the Banana Pi in the upcoming form.

6. Make sure that the **Port forwarding enable for** checkbox is checked.

7. Select **Other applications** within the select box.

8. Enter the name of your new port forwarding rule `Banana Pi HTTPS`.

9. Leave the TCP protocol.

10. Enter port `443` in both the from and to ports.

11. Select the target computer, that is our Banana Pi with the hostname `lemaker`

12. Enter the target port of your Banana Pi that is also `443`.

The following screenshot shows the port forwarding configuration on the Fritz!Box administration interface:

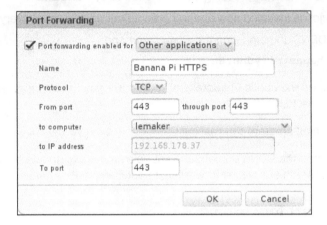

13. Apply the changes by clicking on **OK**.

The new port forwarding rule for the HTTPS port to the Banana Pi is set up. You can now access the Banana Pi from the Internet using your DDNS domain and the HTTPS protocol `https://bananapi.ydns.eu`.

Installing ownCloud

The application ownCloud is a web application just like WordPress or PhpMyAdmin. Therefore, we require a configured web server, database server, and the PHP interpreter. As we have done in a previous recipe, we can move on with the installing of ownCloud.

1. Open a shell on your Banana Pi.

2. Install the required PHP modules:

   ```
   $ sudo apt-get install php5-gd php5-curl
   ```

3. Change to the HTTP root directory:

   ```
   $ cd /usr/share/nginx/www/
   ```

4. Download the ownCloud archive:

   ```
   $ wget https://download.owncloud.org/community/owncloud-
   8.0.2.zip
   ```

 You may want to download a newer version of ownCloud. Visit `https://owncloud.org/changelog/` to determine the current version.

5. Once your download is finished, unpack the archive:

   ```
   $ unzip owncloud-8.0.2.zip
   ```

6. After some time, the archive is unpacked.

7. Create a directory for the data that is synchronized by ownCloud:

   ```
   $ mkdir owncloud/data
   ```

8. Change the owner of the ownCloud directory to the `www-data` user and give proper permissions to that directory:

   ```
   $ sudo chown -R www-data.www-data owncloud/data
   $ sudo chmod 0770 owncloud/data
   ```

9. Create a new database. We can use PhpMyAdmin or the MySQL command line:

   ```
   $ mysql -u root -p
   ```

10. In the MySQL command line, use following commands:

    ```
    mysql> CREATE DATABASE owncloud;
    mysql> GRANT ALL PRIVILEGES ON owncloud.* TO
    owncloud@localhost IDENTIFIED BY 'owncloud_password';
    mysql> FLUSH PRIVILEGES;
    mysql> exit
    ```

11. For Nginx, we need to create a new *virtual* host. Create a new virtual host with an editor like nano using the following command:

    ```
    $ sudo nano /etc/nginx/sites-available/owncloud
    ```

12. The upcoming code is the complete virtual host configuration for our upcoming ownCloud setup. You are able to download the complete configuration from the Packt Publishing website.

13. Start with a new `server` section, defining the new virtual host, the used port, hostname, SSL certificate, and HTTPS directory:

    ```
    server {
            listen 443 ssl;
            server_name bananapi.ydns.eu;
            ssl_certificate /etc/ssl/lemaker.crt;
            ssl_certificate_key /etc/ssl/lemaker.key;

            root /usr/share/nginx/www/owncloud/;
    ```

14. Add configuration options of allowed file size and buffers:

    ```
    client_max_body_size 10G;
    fastcgi_buffers 64 4K;
    ```

15. Add the following rewrite rules to enable shorter URLs later:

```
rewrite ^/caldav(.*)$ /remote.php/caldav$1 redirect;
rewrite ^/carddav(.*)$ /remote.php/carddav$1 redirect;
rewrite ^/webdav(.*)$ /remote.php/webdav$1 redirect;
```

16. Define the index and error pages:

```
index index.php;
error_page 403 /core/templates/403.php;
error_page 404 /core/templates/404.php;
```

17. Permit public access to `robots.txt` to disallow search engines to scan your ownCloud setup:

```
location = /robots.txt {
    allow all;
    log_not_found off;
    access_log off;
}
```

18. Deny direct access to the ownCloud data directory, configurations, and the like:

```
location ~ ^/(data|config|\.ht|db_structure\.xml|README) {
        deny all;
}
```

19. Add general purpose ownCloud rewrite rules:

```
location / {
        rewrite ^/.well-known/host-meta /public.php?service=host-
meta last;
        rewrite ^/.well-known/host-meta.json /public.
php?service=host-meta-json last;

        rewrite ^/.well-known/carddav /remote.php/carddav/
redirect;
        rewrite ^/.well-known/caldav /remote.php/caldav/ redirect;

        rewrite ^(/core/doc/[^\/]+/)$ $1/index.html;

        try_files $uri $uri/ index.php;
}
```

20. Add the PHP configuration:

```
location ~ ^(.+?\.php)(/.*)?$ {
        try_files $1 = 404;

        include fastcgi_params;
        fastcgi_param SCRIPT_FILENAME $document_root$1;
        fastcgi_param PATH_INFO $2;
        fastcgi_param HTTPS on;
        fastcgi_pass unix:/var/run/php5-fpm.sock;
}
```

21. At the end of our configuration, disable the logging of asset files, set the expiration date to 30 days, and close the `server` section with the last curly bracket:

```
location ~*
  ^.+\.(jpg|jpeg|gif|bmp|ico|png|css|js|swf)$ {
        expires 30d;
        # Optional: Don't log access to assets
        access_log off;
    }
}
```

22. Exit and save nano by pressing *Ctrl + X*, followed by *Y* and *Enter*.

23. To enable the newly created virtual host, create a symbolic link (symlink) to `/etc/nginx/sites-enabled/owncloud`:

$ sudo ln -s /etc/nginx/sites-available/owncloud /etc/nginx/sites-enabled/owncloud

24. Restart Nginx to apply the changes:

$ sudo /etc/init.d/nginx restart

25. On your computer, open a browser and go to `https://bananapi.ydns.eu`.

26. Enter a desired username and password for an ownCloud admin. Also, enter the database information that we just created, for example:

   ❑ Username: `admin`
   ❑ Password: `bananapi`
   ❑ Data folder: Leave it as `/usr/share/nginx/www/owncloud/data`
   ❑ Database user: `owncloud`
   ❑ Database password: `owncloud_password`
   ❑ Database name: `owncloud`
   ❑ Database host: `localhost`

The following screenshot shows the final steps of the ownCloud setup:

27. Finish the setup by clicking on **Finish setup**.

You have set up ownCloud successfully and will be welcomed by its web interface.

How it works...

To synchronize files over the Internet, we need to permit access to the Banana Pi from the Internet. Therefore, we need to know either our public IP address, which may change from time to time, or alternatively, set up a DDNS domain. By using a DDNS domain, we get a domain name that never changes. Still the DDNS service has to know the current public IP address to resolve the address correctly. This is why we need to update our DDNS domain periodically. In this recipe, we are updating the DDNS domain via a shell script. A shell script is a set of commands that are executed by the shell. The first line of a script that is interpreted by the shell should be the so-called shebang (`#!/bin/bash`). It indicates which shell or interpreter has to be used when running this script (`/bin/bash` in our case).

The next three lines in our script are *shell* variables. Variables can be used later in the script as we do in the last line:

```
curl --user $USER:$PASS https://ydns.eu/api/v1/update/?host=$HOST
```

The preceding line executes the `curl` command that does an HTTPS request to the yDNS update URL. The curl program is quite similar to the wget program. It can also download files from web servers and the like. In fact, we can also solve the task with wget. We are using curl in this recipe for educational and convenience reasons.

The resulting URL from our previous `curl` command is:

```
https://ydns.eu/api/v1/update/?host=bananapi.ydns.eu
```

Note that the string `$HOST` is replaced with the `HOST` variable by the shell. Thus, a variable is *declared* without the dollar sign ($) and *used* with the dollar sign. This URL is our yDNS update URL. As only logged in users are allowed to update specific DDNS domains, we have to provide the login information when doing that HTTPS request. This is what the parameter `--user` followed by the username and password separated by the colon does. As we are using variables here as well, the resulting parameter is:

```
--user my_email@my_provider.com:bananapi
```

As scripts need to be executable, we are using the `chmod a+x` command. You remember that the `a+x` parameter means for *all* (a) *add* (+) *execute* (x) permissions. We are testing the shell script using the full path as a command:

```
$ /home/bananapi/scripts/ydns_update.sh
```

As we need to update the IP address for our domain frequently, we are creating a cron job. Cron is a scheduler that is a utility to run jobs (tasks and commands) periodically at fixed times. In our case, we are repeating our update shell script every 15 minutes. To create a cron job, the crontab (cron table) has to be edited. This can be done using the command `crontab -e`.

The parameter `-e` means edit. To list all current cron jobs, you can use `crontab -l`.

Each cron job is a line in the crontab. We added the following line:

```
*/15 * * * * /home/bananapi/scripts/ydns_update.sh
```

The first five parts are the definition of the repeating period. As our first part is `*/15`, it means every 15 minutes. If you make it `*` only, the task will be repeated every minute. The next four stars mean every hour, every day, every month, and every week. The last parameter is the command that has to be executed when the time event occurs. After saving the crontab, the cron job is installed and triggered according to our period definition automatically.

Your router will usually block any requests from the Internet to your local area network for security reasons. To permit accessing to a specific service, we need to forward a port from the router to the Banana Pi. As we want to use the secure HTTPS protocol only to access our ownCloud solution, we open the HTTPS port 443 on the router and forward it to port 443 on the Banana Pi. Your router will route HTTPS requests from the Internet to the Banana Pi. Keep in mind, that any other protocol (including normal HTTP, port 80) will still be blocked until you forward these ports as well.

The ownCloud application requires a configured database and a specific configuration of our web server. To separate this configuration from our normal Nginx configuration, we use a feature called **virtual hosts**. Virtual hosting is a mechanism to use multiple domains on our single web server. This way, the Nginx web server will handle requests to `lemaker` differently than to `bananapi.ydns.eu`. For `lemaker`, the configuration from the previous recipe is used. However, if requests are going to the `bananapi.ydns.eu` domain, Nginx determines the virtual host configuration from `/etc/nginx/sites-available/owncloud`.

Nginx determines the configuration that is to be used according to the `server_name` option in the configuration. The `server_name` option has to match with the `Host` field of an HTTP request. You can see that the ownCloud configuration file has the value of the `bananapi.ydns.eu` domain as `server_name`. You can also see that we are using `/usr/share/nginx/www/owncloud/` as the HTTP root for that domain. Also, our SSL key and certificate from the previous recipe is used. Most of the other configuration options within that file are options that are mostly for security or convenience reasons recommended by the official ownCloud documentation.

To actually enable the created virtual host, we have to add a symbolic link (symlink) to `/etc/nginx/sites-enabled/`. After a restart of the Nginx web server, the new virtual host is ready. Keep in mind that we used our previously created SSL certificate that is issued for the hostname (common name) `lemaker`. This means some applications such as Internet Explorer will warn you about the mismatched address. Therefore, it is recommended to create and configure a correct SSL certificate with the common name `bananapi.ydns.eu`.

Once the virtual host configuration and the database is set up for ownCloud, we can finish the ownCloud installation by browsing to the URL `https://bananapi.ydns.eu` for the first time. You then enter your desired administrator account details for ownCloud.

When this is finished, you have successfully set up your ownCloud solution. You can now upload and download files from or to your ownCloud.

There's more...

There are several ways to access your ownCloud application. You can use the web interface by browsing to our ownCloud URL. Alternatively, you can use the official ownCloud client that is provided by the developers of ownCloud for several operating systems. This is recommended if you want to have automatic synchronization just like with the Dropbox application.

Furthermore, ownCloud supports apps. For example, you can enable calendar and contacts apps, which support the CalDAV and CardDAV protocol. Using CalDAV and CardDAV, you are able to synchronize contacts and calendar entries with your cell phone.

There are a lot of possibilities with your ownCloud setup. Refer to the official documentation on how to use all these opportunities.

The following steps explain how to install and configure the ownCloud client on Windows:

1. Open a browser and go to `https://owncloud.org/install/#install-clients`.
2. Click on the **Windows** box to choose to download the Windows client.
3. Once the download is finished, run the downloaded installer.
4. In the **ownCloud Setup** window, click on **Next**.
5. Select the **Standard** type of installation and click on **Next**.
6. Choose a directory to install the client into or stay with the default. Click on **Install**.
7. Once the installation is completed, click on **Next**.
8. Leave **Run ownCloud** checked, and click on **Finish**.
9. The **ownCloud Connection Wizard** opens.
10. Enter the ownCloud **Server Address** as `https://bananapi.ydns.eu`.
11. An **SSL Connection** windows will open, warning you about the SSL certificate. It is quite the same warning that is discussed in the previous recipe. Check the **Trust this certificate anyway** box and click on **OK**.
12. The next step asks for the ownCloud credentials. Enter the credentials you chose while the ownCloud setup, for example:
    - Username: `admin`
    - Password: `bananapi`
13. In the upcoming local folder options, you can choose what you want to synchronize and in which directory you want to synchronize your files. You may want to select **Sync everything from server** and change the **Local folder** to your desired target directory.
14. Click on **Connect** followed by **Finish**.

The synchronization process begins and after some time your files will be synchronized with the directory you chose in the client setup. You can place any file or directory into your chosen ownCloud directory and it will be synchronized automatically with your ownCloud account.

To enable or disable certain apps, log in to the ownCloud web interface as administrator and click on **Files** (upper-left corner) and click on **Apps** in the upcoming menu. On the **Apps** page, there are several apps available. For example, the **Calendar** and **Contacts** apps are found under **PIM** in the right menu. To use the CalDAV and CardDAV features, you need to have these ownCloud apps enabled.

On Linux, there are several ways in which to install the ownCloud client. The easiest way on Debian-based distributions is via Apt:

```
$ sudo apt-get install owncloud-client
```

Once you install the client, you can start it by using the `owncloud` command. When starting the ownCloud client for the first time, you will be directed through the same configuration wizard like on the Windows operating system (see above).

See also

  ▶ Find a user manual, an administrator manual, and a developer manual at the official ownCloud documentation available at `https://doc.owncloud.org/`

  ▶ The Wikipedia article about the Cron scheduler at `https://en.wikipedia.org/wiki/Cron`

  ▶ A great tutorial about shell scripting—*Bash Shell Scripting* on Wikibooks at `https://en.wikibooks.org/wiki/Bash_Shell_Scripting`

Controlling the desktop remotely using VNC

The **VNC** (**Virtual Network Computing**) system is a great choice if you need to control your LXDE desktop remotely. In this recipe, we are discovering how to install a VNC server and connect to the Banana Pi using a VNC client.

Getting ready

The following ingredients are required to build a VNC server on the Banana Pi:

  ▶ A running Banana Pi with a Debian-based Linux system

  ▶ A configured network on the Banana Pi

How to do it...

We are going to install the VNC server onto our Banana Pi and access the Banana Pi remotely via a VNC client.

Installing the VNC server on the Banana Pi

Installing and running the VNC server is quite simple:

1. Open a shell.
2. Install the `x11vnc` package:

```
$ sudo apt-get install x11vnc
```

3. Apt will ask you to confirm the installation of the dependency packages.

4. Enter Y to continue the installation.

   After a few seconds to minutes, the VNC server is installed.

5. Run the VNC server:

   ```
   $ x11vnc -display :0
   ```

The VNC server will start and you can access it via a VNC client.

Installing and using a VNC client on Windows

On Windows, there exists several VNC clients. The TightVNC client is recommended.

 Make sure that the VNC server is running on the Banana Pi. The VNC server will shut down, once you close a client session.

1. On your Windows system, open a browser and go to:
   http://tightvnc.com/download.php.

2. Download the installer for your system architecture and run the application.

3. Click on **Next** twice.

4. Select **Custom** as the setup type.

5. We only need the VNC viewer (the client) on our computer. Therefore, click on the icon that is to the left of **TightVNC Server** and select **Entire feature will be unavailable** in the upcoming menu.

6. Click on **Next**.

7. In the **Additional Tasks**, it is recommended that you leave both the checkboxes enabled.

8. Finally, click on **Install** to install the TightVNC client and finish the installer by clicking on **Finish**.

9. Open the installed VNC client named TightVNC Viewer.

10. Enter the IP address or the hostname of the Banana Pi as remote host, for example, lemaker.

11. Click on **Connect**.

The VNC client will open a window containing the complete LXDE desktop of your Banana Pi; refer to the following screenshot:

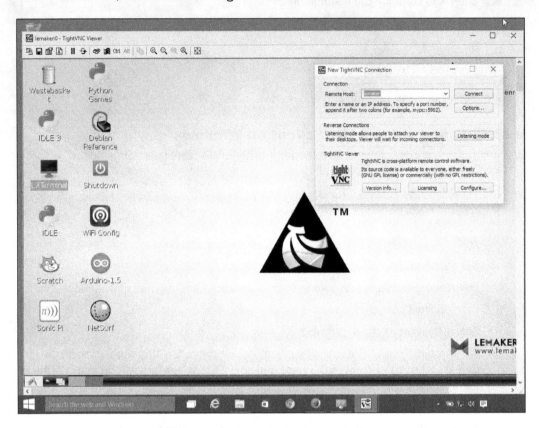

You have now successfully connected to your Banana Pi's desktop.

Installing and using a VNC client on Linux

On Linux operating systems, you can use your distribution's package manager to install a VNC client. Mostly, you will be fine by installing the vncviewer application.

 Make sure that the VNC server is running on the Banana Pi. The VNC server will shut down once you close a client session.

1. Within your Debian-based distribution, open a shell.
2. Install the vncviewer program:

```
$ sudo apt-get install vncviewer
```

3. Open the vncviwer application with the hostname or IP address of the Banana Pi as argument:

    ```
    $ vncviewer lemaker
    ```

4. The VNC client will open a window containing the desktop of your Banana Pi.

You have now successfully connected to your Banana Pi's desktop.

How it works...

Setting up a VNC server on the Banana Pi is easy. You need the x11vnc application, run it, and connect to your Banana Pi remotely via a VNC client.

When running the VNC server, we used the parameter `-display :0`. This means we acquire the picture of the first X11 display. That is the so-called *root display*. It is exactly the picture that is shown when connecting your Banana Pi to a display. You can try to omit the `display` parameter or change the used value, but it may result in a failure while starting the VNC.

The VNC client on the other hand tries to connect using the VNC protocol. When connecting successfully, it will show the picture of the X11 root display within a new opened window. You can control your desktop just like you would directly via the attached keyboard, mouse, and monitor.

There's more...

Once your VNC server is running, everyone on your local network can connect to the Banana Pi using a VNC client. To avoid that, you can secure your VNC server with a password file. To do that, we need to create a password file first:

```
$ x11vnc -storepasswd
```

You will be requested to enter a desired VNC password twice and to confirm the default location of the created password file. Confirm by entering `Y` and your VNC server is password protected in the future when running with the `-rfbauth` parameter:

```
$ x11vnc -display :0 -rfbauth /home/bananapi/.vnc/passwd
```

The `-forever` parameter will preserve the VNC server session when you close your client. The `-shared` parameter will allow multiple VNC client sessions simultaneously.

Therefore, after creating a VNC password file, you can start your server like this:

```
$ x11vnc -display :0 -rfbauth /home/bananapi/.vnc/passwd -forever -shared
```

To stop the VNC server you need to press *Ctrl + C*.

You can connect to your Banana Pi over the Internet when you set up a DDNS domain (as seen in the previous recipe) and forward the VNC port 5900 to your Banana Pi. However, the VNC protocol is *not encrypted*. Therefore, it is strongly recommended to avoid connecting directly to your VNC server over the Internet as every mouse and keyboard input is transmitted in cleartext.

You can still use VNC over an encrypted channel by using a so-called SSH tunnel. The SSH protocol, which we discovered in *Chapter 2, Administration*, is able to forward ports over SSH from the client to the server (also the other way round). This way you are able to securely use VNC over the encrypted SSH connection.

Adding a SSH tunnel for VNC in PuTTY

To add an SSH tunnel in PuTTY, you need to do the following:

1. Open PuTTY.
2. Click on your Banana Pi profile in **Saved Sessions** and click on **Load**.
3. Navigate to **Connection | SSH | Tunnels**.
4. For **Source port**, enter 5900.
5. For **Destination**, enter localhost:5900.
6. Click on **Add**.
7. Return to **Session**.
8. Save the changes to your **Saved Session** profile.
9. Open the connection to your Banana Pi.

When successfully connected via SSH, your tunnel is established. To use VNC over the encrypted SSH tunnel, use the hostname localhost instead of lemaker in the VNC client. PuTTY will tunnel the port 5900 from your local machine (that is localhost) over the encrypted SSH connection to the Banana Pi.

If you enabled port forwarding to your Banana Pi for SSH in your router settings, you can also use VNC via that SSH tunnel over the Internet. Refer to the following recipe for enhanced security when using SSH over the Internet.

Using an SSH tunnel for VNC on Linux

On your Linux computer, you can establish an SSH tunnel easily via a parameter when using the ssh command or via the ~/.ssh/config we introduced in *Chapter 2, Administration*.

When connecting to your Banana Pi with the -L parameter, you create an SSH tunnel:

```
$ ssh -L 5900:localhost:5900 bananapi@lemaker
```

Alternatively, you can persist the tunnel by adding the following to your client's SSH configuration file:

```
$ nano ~/.ssh/config
```

Also add the `LocalForward` option to your Banana Pi host configuration:

```
Host lemaker
    HostName lemaker
    User bananapi
    LocalForward 5900 localhost:5900
```

When connecting to the Banana Pi via SSH, you establish an SSH tunnel to port 5900. You can connect to the Banana Pi's VNC server via `vncviewer localhost`. The VNC connection is encrypted using that SSH tunnel.

See also

- The Wikipedia article about Virtual Network Computing at `https://en.wikipedia.org/wiki/Virtual_Network_Computing`

- The official website of the TightVNC application set at `http://tightvnc.com`

- The website of the x11vnc VNC server at `http://www.karlrunge.com/x11vnc/`

- The *SSH Tunneling Explained* article—a useful guide on how SSH tunneling works and how to use it at `https://chamibuddhika.wordpress.com/2012/03/21/ssh-tunnelling-explained/`

Securing SSH using SSH keys

You can use SSH over the Internet by opening a port in your router configuration just as it is demonstrated in the *Synchronizing files over the Internet* recipe. When doing so, your Banana Pi's SSH server is accessible over the Internet. This means that everybody is able to log in to your Banana Pi. This is especially risky if you have not changed the default password.

There are several methods to improve the security of your SSH server on the Internet. The three most used methods are:

- You use a different port. For example, you could use port 22222 instead of the default 22. This will keep away a lot of potential attackers using superficial port scanners.

- You disable the password login to your SSH server by using SSH keys as the authentication method.

▸ You disable the possibility to log in as root by setting the variable `PermitRootLogin` to `no` in the `/etc/ssh/sshd_config` file.

In this recipe, we are going present the second method. Thus, we generate SSH keys and disable the password login. This will enhance the security of your SSH so that you can use SSH to your Banana Pi over the Internet.

Getting ready

The following ingredients are required on your Banana Pi:

▸ A running Banana Pi with a Debian-based Linux system

▸ A configured network on the Banana Pi

▸ A configured SSH server

▸ To generate the required key pair, you will need PuTTYGen on your Windows computer or the ssh-keygen application on your Linux computer.

How to do it...

You will have to generate an SSH key pair for your SSH client. Afterwards, we need to store the generated public key on the Banana Pi to be recognizable by the SSH server. After we configured the key authentication on both the Banana Pi and the client, we can disable the SSH password login.

Using SSH keys in PuTTY

On Windows, you can use the tool PuTTYGen to generate an SSH key pair. The PuTTYGen utility is packed within the `putty.zip` we presented in *Chapter 2, Administration*. Let's see how this can be done:

1. Start the PuTTYGen application by running the `PuTTYGen.exe` file.

2. Click on the **Generate** button.

3. While the key pair is generated, move the mouse randomly over the blank area.

4. After the generation, you will see your public key within the text area.

5. To protect your private key, enter a **Key passphrase** and repeat it in the **Confirm passphrase** text field, for example, `bananapi`.

6. The passphrase is like a password for your private key. This way you protect your private key in case someone gains access to it.

7. Save your private key by clicking on **Save private key**, selecting a target directory, and entering the filename `private.ppk`.

8. Copy the whole public key by marking the complete text on the text area above **Key fingerprint** and pressing *Ctrl + C* or by right-clicking on it and then clicking on **Copy**.

9. The next step is to paste the public key into `/home/bananapi/.ssh/authorized_keys` on your Banana Pi.

10. Open the normal PuTTY application and connect to your Banana Pi.

11. Create the `~/.ssh` directory, if it does not exist right now, and set access permissions for the current user only:

   ```
   $ mkdir ~/.ssh
   $ chmod 700 ~/.ssh
   ```

12. Edit `~/.ssh/authorized_keys` using an editor like nano:

   ```
   $ nano /home/bananapi/.ssh/authorized_keys
   ```

13. Paste the copied public key by right-clicking on the nano editor:

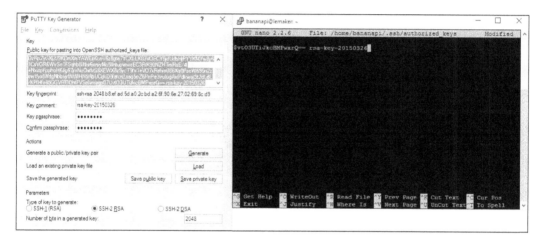

14. In the preceding screenshot you can see the selected public key within PuTTYGen. This public key is then pasted into `~/.ssh/authorized_keys` using nano.

15. Exit and save nano by pressing *Ctrl + X*, followed by *Y* and *Enter*.

16. Close the SSH session by pressing *Ctrl + D* or entering the `exit` command.

The public key generated from PuTTYGen is now an authorized key. This means, you can connect using your private key and your passphrase from now on. Configure PuTTY to use the private key as the authentication method by following these steps:

1. Reopen the normal PuTTY application.

2. Click on your Banana Pi profile in **Saved Sessions** and click on **Load**.

3. Navigate to **Connection | SSH | Auth** on the right menu.

4. Click on **Browse** next to the **Private key file for authentication** text field.

5. Select the `private.ppk` key file you generated previously.

6. Return to **Session**.

7. Save the changes to your **Saved Session** profile.

8. Open the connection to your Banana Pi.

9. Instead of requesting the SSH password, PuTTY will ask you for the passphrase to unlock your private key.

10. Enter the passphrase that you chose after generating the private key. In our example, we used the passphrase `bananapi`.

You are logged in successfully using the more secure SSH key authentication.

Using SSH keys on Linux

On Linux systems, you can use the ssh-keygen tool to generate a key pair.

1. On your Linux computer, open a shell.

2. Generate a key pair:

```
$ ssh-keygen -t rsa
```

3. You will be asked where to save the private key. Confirm the default by pressing *Enter*.

4. Type a passphrase to protect your private key; for example, `bananapi`.

5. Enter the same passphrase again.

6. Your private key is stored under `~/.ssh/id_rsa` and your public key is stored under `~/.ssh/id_rsa.pub`.

7. Transfer the public key to the Banana Pi using the `ssh-copy-id` command:

```
$ ssh-copy-id bananapi@lemaker
```

8. You will be prompted to use the SSH password to transfer the public key. Enter the SSH password.

9. Use the `-i` (identity) parameter, to start an SSH connection using your private key:

```
$ ssh -i ~/.ssh/id_rsa bananapi@lemaker
```

10. You should be able to log in to your Banana Pi when entering your private key's passphrase.

You are logged in successfully using the more secure SSH key authentication. On your client computer, you can now configure the used private key by appending an `IdentityFile` option to your host configuration in `~/.ssh/config`:

```
Host lemaker
   HostName lemaker
   User bananapi
   IdentityFile ~/.ssh/id_rsa
```

Disabling the SSH password login on the Banana Pi

Once we are able to log in to the Banana Pi via the SSH key authentication, we can disable the password login.

Make sure that you are able to log in via your private key; otherwise, you may lock out yourself. In this case, you have to turn off your Banana Pi, insert the SD card into a Linux computer, and restore the default `sshd_config` file on the SD card. Therefore, we are creating a backup of the default file in the following steps:

1. Open a shell on your Banana Pi.

2. Make a backup of the default `/etc/ssh/sshd_config`:

   `$ sudo cp /etc/ssh/sshd_config /etc/ssh/sshd_config.backup`

3. Edit `/etc/ssh/sshd_config`:

   `$ sudo nano /etc/ssh/sshd_config`

4. Press *Ctrl + W* to open a search dialog.

5. Type `PasswordAuthentication` into the search field and hit *Enter*.

6. You will be directed to the commented out `PasswordAuthentication` option.

7. Remove the comment (delete the # character) and change the value to `no`. It should look as shown in the next screenshot:

   ```
   # Change to no to disable tunnelled clear text passwords
   PasswordAuthentication no
   ```

8. Exit and save nano by pressing *Ctrl + X*, followed by *Y* and *Enter*.

9. Restart the SSH server:

   `$ sudo /etc/init.d/ssh restart`

10. Exit the SSH session by typing *Ctrl + D* or using the `exit` command.

You should be able to log in using your private key as the authentication method only.

You can test it by forcing a password login on your Linux computer or removing the private key file in your PuTTY settings, for example:

1. On your Linux computer, try to force a password login via the options (-o) parameter:

   ```
   $ ssh -o PubkeyAuthentication=no bananapi@lemaker
   ```

2. You should see an error `Permission denied (publickey)`.

3. Now try to log in via the private key:

   ```
   $ ssh -i ~/.ssh/id_rsa bananapi@lemaker
   ```

4. You should be able to log in after entering your correct passphrase.

You have successfully enhanced security by enabling the SSH key authentication.

How it works...

In this recipe, we enabled the SSH authentication via an SSH key pair. A key pair consists of a public key and a private key (similar to the key pair we created for the SSL certificate). The client's public key can be stored on multiple SSH servers. The private key will remain on the client's machine.

When a client connects to the SSH server using his private key, the server checks whether the client's public key is stored on the server. If this is the case, the user has to enter the passphrase of his private key to unlock it.

The passphrase provides optional additional security. Imagine an attacker gaining access to your private key file. If you had no passphrase on your key file, the attacker could log in to your Banana Pi by just using that hijacked private key. However, as we secured our private key with the passphrase, the attack must have both your private key file and your passphrase to unlock it.

The private and public keys are generated by utilities such as PuTTYGen on Windows or ssh-keygen on Linux. You can store your public key on every SSH server that you have access to and log in via your private key. The private key, however, should be stored safely on your client's computer.

To log in via the SSH key authentication mechanism, you have to tell your SSH client (that is PuTTY or the `ssh` command) to use a private key file (the identity file). On PuTTY, you have to select the private key in the settings. The `ssh` command on Linux can take the `-i` (identity) parameter or use a host configuration in `~/.ssh/config`.

Once we are able to log in via our SSH keys, we can disable the SSH password login completely. When this is done, you can safely establish a port forwarding in your router to the Banana Pi and log in from the Internet. Keep in mind that you will need to have your private key to log in.

If you want to add another public key, you can only add it if you log in with a previously permitted private key.

See also

▸ A great Wiki article about SSH keys in general—*SSH keys* on Arch Linux wiki at `https://wiki.archlinux.org/index.php/SSH_keys`

Setting up a UPnP media server

In this final recipe, we are going to set up a UPnP media server. In this case, it is the DLNA server MiniDLNA (also known as ReadyMedia). For legibility reasons, we are using the old term *MiniDLNA*.

Getting ready

The following ingredients are required for our upcoming DLNA server:

▸ A running Banana Pi with a Debian-based Linux system
▸ A configured network on the Banana Pi

How to do it...

Setting up MiniDLNA is relatively simple. As always, you need to install the required package and configure some parameters. Let's do it:

1. Open a shell on your Banana Pi.
2. We are going to place our media files like video or audio files into a directory on our external HDD. Therefore, we create a new media directory on our NTFS partition. Make sure, that the HDD is mounted:

```
$ mkdir /mnt/ntfs_partition/media
```

3. Place some media files into that new directory, for example, the free *Big Buck Bunny* movie:

```
$ cd /mnt/ntfs_partition/media
$ wget http://mirrorblender.top-ix.org/
peach/bigbuckbunny_movies/big_buck_bunny_720p_surround.avi
```

4. Install the MiniDLNA server:

```
$ sudo apt-get install minidlna
```

5. Edit /etc/minidlna.conf with an editor like nano:

```
$ sudo nano /etc/minidlna.conf
```

6. You will find a lot of documentation comments. Edit at least the media_dir option. We can also add friendly_name to identify our Banana Pi.

```
media_dir=/mnt/ntfs_partition/media
friendly_name=Banana Pi MiniDLNA server
```

7. Exit and save nano by pressing *Ctrl* + *X*, followed by *Y* and *Enter*.

8. Reload the MiniDLNA server:

```
$ sudo /etc/init.d/minidlna force-reload
```

9. MiniDLNA will scan the media directory.

10. On your computer, open a browser and go to http://lemaker:8200.

You should see the status of your MiniDLNA server, for example, as shown in the next screenshot:

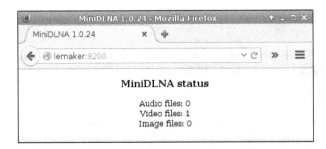

If you see a screenshot similar to the previous one, your DLNA server is set up and configured. You can stream your media files with any media player that is DLNA compatible. For example, the Windows Media Player is able to play DLNA content. The previous screenshot shows the Windows Media Player listing the *Big Buck Bunny* movie from our Banana Pi's MiniDLNA server:

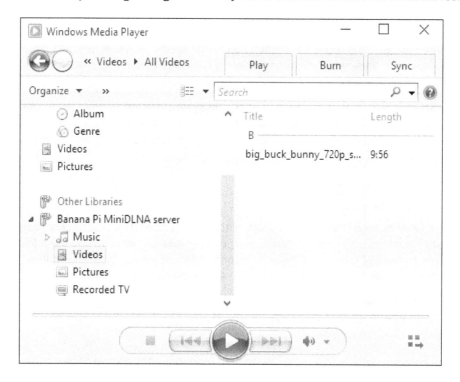

How it works...

DLNA stands for Digital Living Network Alliance and is the organization that defines standard guidelines for sharing digital media between multimedia devices. UPnP on the other hand stands for Universal Plug and Play and is a set of networking protocols to discover UPnP-compliant devices on a network. By setting up a UPnP media server such as MiniDLNA, we can stream various media files such as videos, music, photos, and so forth from our Banana Pi to any UPnP respectively DLNA-compatible client.

In this recipe, we assume that we have a mounted partition under `/mnt/ntfs_partition` as explained in *Chapter 3, External Disks*. In that partition, we created a new directory to put our future media files into. To test our MiniDLNA setup, we downloaded a video called *Big Buck Bunny* using the wget program into that media directory. It is a computer animated open source comedy short film, which we can download and use for free.

Once we have one or more media files within our media directory, we can set up the UPnP server MiniDLNA. Therefore, we installed it via Apt and configured MiniDLNA by editing its configuration file (`/etc/minidlna.conf`).

It is only required to enter the directory containing the media files (option `media_dir`), but we also assigned a name (option `friendly_name`) to recognize the server on the network easily.

To apply the changes, it is required to restart the UPnP server. However, restarting the server using the `restart` parameter would not initiate a rescan of the changed media directory. Therefore, we used the force-reload parameter instead.

Once the MiniDLNA is started, the built-in HTTP server provides information about the scanned media via a browser. As the default HTTP port (port 80) is usually used by dedicated web servers (such as our Nginx), MiniDLNA uses the port 8200 per default. Therefore, you can access the MiniDLNA server with the URL `http://lemaker:8200`.

There's more...

You have a lot of options that you can modify within `/etc/minidlna.conf`. For example, it is possible to distinguish audio, video, and picture directories. You can use the `A` (audio), `V` (video), or `P` (picture) prefixes followed by a comma before your `media_dir` values. You can also define more than one media directory. See the following example:

```
media_dir=A,/mnt/ntfs_partition/audio
media_dir=V,/mnt/ntfs_partition/videos
media_dir=P,/mnt/ntfs_partition/pictures
```

For all the possible options, it is recommended to read the manual page of the MiniDLNA configuration:

```
$ man minidlna.conf
```

Note that our MiniDLNA server does not transcode content. Transcoding means to convert the files before streaming (for example, an MP3 file to a WAV stream).Thus, your DLNA client has to support the format you want to stream. Furthermore, transcoding requires extreme computing performance.

There still exists a fork (a customized version) of MiniDLNA that supports transcoding. If you are interested in transcoding, you can try to compile the fork called ReadyMedia-transcode for yourself. Instructions are found on the website of that fork at `https://bitbucket.org/stativ/readymedia-transcode/`.

See also

> ▶ The official website of MiniDLNA also known as ReadyMedia
>   `http://minidlna.sourceforge.net/`

5

Using the GPIO Pins

In this chapter, we will cover the following recipes:

- ▸ Lighting up an LED using the gpio command
- ▸ Programming the LED
- ▸ Using the GPIO input with a pushbutton

Introduction

This chapter covers the basics of the hardware world of the Banana Pi. Just like the Raspberry Pi and the Arduino, the Banana Pi is able to interact with external electrical components. To achieve this, we are going to use the **GPIO** (**General-Purpose input/output**) pins that are introduced in this chapter.

We will switch on an LED using the shell and with a small application that we are programming. Furthermore, we will build a circuit, including a pull-down resistor and control an LED with a button. To achieve this, we will introduce the C programming language with the `WiringPi` library and the Python scripting language with the `RPi.GPIO` library.

Lighting up an LED using the gpio command

This recipe is the "Hello World"equivalent of electrical experiments with a single-board computer. We will connect an LED to a GPIO pin of the Banana Pi and apply a logical high signal on that pin. This will enlighten the LED.

Getting ready

We require several components to switch on an LED on the Banana Pi:

- A Linux system on the Banana Pi
- Access to the shell
- A 5mm LED (forward voltage 2.0 V)
- A 470 Ω resistor
- A breadboard
- Two female to male jumper wires

You can conveniently purchase these components at retailers that specialize in electronics. Most of the components in this and the upcoming recipes are available for a low price.

How to do it...

The following steps will switch on an LED. You will find the complete Banana Pi and Banana Pro pin layout in the *There's more...* section of this recipe.

 Before you connect or disconnect any electrical parts, *power off your Banana Pi* and also *unplug the power supply*.

1. Connect the first jumper wire to the GPIO 1 pin. That is the physical pin 12.
2. Connect the other end of the first jumper wire to your breadboard.
3. Attach the resistor to the same row on the breadboard.
4. Plug in the LED to the breadboard. Pay attention to the polarity of the LED. The anode has to direct to the resistor while the cathode directs to the ground (GND). Use a different row on your breadboard for the cathode.
5. Close the circuit by attaching the second jumper wire on the same row as the cathode of the LED and connect the other end to a GND pin on the Banana Pi. For example, you can use the physical pin 14 that is directly under GPIO 1.

The following picture shows the resulting electrical circuit on the Banana Pi:

The same electrical circuit is shown as a graphical illustration:

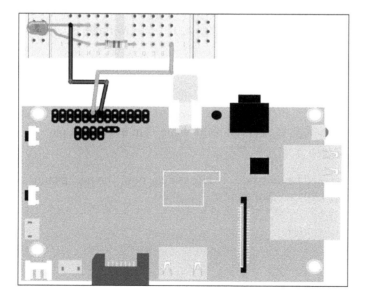

6. Power on your Banana Pi.

   Once the Banana Pi is booted up, we need to build WiringPi to control the pin headers.

7. Open a shell and switch to the home directory:

   ```
   $ cd ~
   ```

8. Download the source code from the GitHub repository:

   ```
   $ git clone https://github.com/LeMaker/WiringBP -b bananapi
   ```

    If you use the Banana Pro, use the following command instead:
   ```
   $ git clone https://github.com/LeMaker/
   WiringBP -b bananapro
   ```

9. If you do not have the build-essential tools installed, install them:

   ```
   $ sudo apt-get install build-essential
   ```

10. Change to the downloaded source code directory and make the build script executable:

    ```
    $ cd ~/WiringBP
    ```
    ```
    $ chmod +x ./build
    ```

11. Run the build script as root:

    ```
    $ sudo ./build
    ```

12. The `WiringPi` library will be compiled. This will take a few seconds to a few minutes.

13. Eventually, you will see the message `All Done`. WiringPi is now installed on your Banana Pi or Banana Pro.

14. We are switching on the LED now. Set the mode of the GPIO 1 pin to the output mode:

    ```
    $ gpio mode 1 OUTPUT
    ```

15. Write a logical high signal (that is the value 1) to the GPIO 1 pin:

    ```
    $ gpio write 1 1
    ```

    Your LED should be switched on successfully now. The next picture shows the enlightened LED on a Banana Pi:

16. To switch off the LED, write a logical low signal (value 0) to the GPIO 1 pin:

```
$ gpio write 1 0
```

How it works...

We built an electrical circuit, including the resistor and the LED in this recipe. Once we are finished building the circuit, we can boot up the Banana Pi.

To enlighten the LED, we are using the gpio command that is part of the package WiringPi. Unfortunately, WiringPi is not provided in the standard repositories; therefore, we are compiling it from source.

Compiling from source is trivial in this case. We download the source code from GitHub, assign executive permissions to the included build script, and run that build script. The build script contains instructions about which files need to be compiled and how. In the end, the compiled libraries and programs are installed on the system, including the gpio program.

Once we have access to the gpio command, we are setting the mode of the GPIO pin number 1. We set the mode to OUTPUT. This instructs the Banana Pi to handle the GPIO 1 pin as an output pin. The next step is to write a logical high signal to that GPIO 1 pin. This will instruct the Banana Pi to apply a voltage of 3.3V at the GPIO 1 pin. The LED begins to shine.

[Keep in mind to not connect devices with another logic voltage such as the Arduino, which applies 5.0V at logic.]

There's more...

On some distributions, the `gpio` program is already shipped. For example, on the Raspbian distribution for the Banana Pi, the WiringPi package is included. Unfortunately, it is compiled for the Banana Pro model only (at least on release version that was released on December 26, 2014). Therefore, we are compiling WiringPi from source to make sure that it works appropriately.

The value of the required resistor is calculated by Ohm's law. See the following equation:

$$R = \frac{V}{I} = \frac{(3.3V - 2.0V)}{\frac{50mA}{17}} = 442\Omega$$

The required resistance (*R*) is calculated by voltage (*V*) divided by current (*I*). The voltage is calculated by the 3.3 V that is applied on the GPIO pin minus the power consumption of the LED (that is usually 2.0 V). The current is calculated by the maximum permitted current draw from the 3.3 V pins (that is 50 mA) divided by the number of available GPIO pins (that is 17). As there exists no 442 Ω resistors, we are using a 470 Ω resistor.

The Banana Pi pin layout

The following pictures show the physical pin numerations for the Banana Pi:

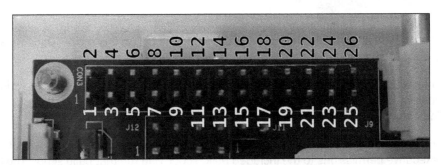

To translate the physical pin numeration into the WiringPi numeration, which is used when executing the `gpio` program, you see the pin layout for the Banana Pi in the next table:

WiringPi	Name	Physical	Physical	Name	WiringPi
	3.3V	1	2	5.0V	
8	SDA	3	4	5.0V	
9	SCL	5	6	GND	
7	GPIO 7	7	8	TxD	15
	GND	9	10	RxD	16

WiringPi	Name	Physical	Physical	Name	WiringPi
0	GPIO 0	11	12	GPIO 1	1
2	GPIO 2	13	14	GND	
3	GPIO 3	15	16	GPIO 4	4
	3.3V	17	18	GPIO 5	5
12	MOSI	19	20	GND	
13	MISO	21	22	GPIO 6	6
14	SCLK	23	24	CE0	10
	GND	25	26	CE1	11

You can see that the physical pin number 12 has the name GPIO 1. It is identified by WiringPi via number 1. The GPIO 5 pin is identified by WiringPi via number 5 and is the 18th physical pin. The positive power-supply pins (1, 2, 4, and 17) and the ground pins (6, 9, 14, 20, and 25) have no WiringPi identifier.

The Banana Pro pin layout

The next picture shows the physical pin numerations for the Banana Pro:

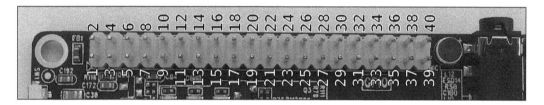

As shown in the preceding picture, the Banana Pro extends the Banana Pi pin layout with 14 more pins. The first 26 pins are identical to the pin layout of the Banana Pi.

The following table illustrates the additional 14 pins of the Banana Pro:

WiringPi	Name	Physical	Physical	Name	WiringPi
30	SDA.0	27	28	SCL.0	31
21	GPIO 21	29	30	GND	
22	GPIO 22	31	32	GPIO 26	26
23	GPIO 23	33	34	GND	
24	GPIO 24	35	36	GPIO 27	27
25	GPIO 25	37	38	GPIO 28	28
	GND	39	40	GPIO 29	29

Using a GPIO extension board

If you experiment a lot with electronic components and the GPIO pins, you may be interested in using a GPIO extension board. It is a convenient addition to your breadboard and Banana Pi:

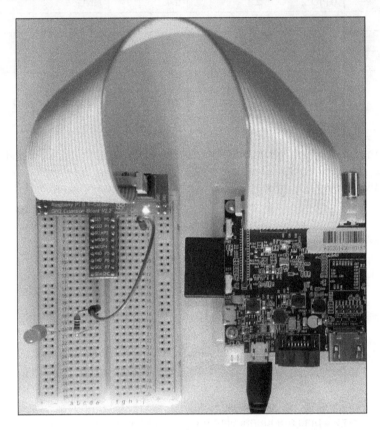

The previous picture shows the same circuit we used in this recipe realized with a GPIO extension board. You see that the resistor is connected via the jumper wire to the same line like the extension board's P1 connection. The P1 connector directs to GPIO 1. On the other hand, the cathode of the LED is connected to the (blue vertical) negative line, which directs to ground.

As most of the Banana Pi's pins are compatible with the Raspberry Pi pins, the power-supply pins in particular, it is possible to use a Raspberry Pi GPIO extension board (as shown in the previous picture). However, some GPIO numerations are different than on the Raspberry Pi. For example, the GPIO 25 pin on the Raspberry Pi (physical pin 22) is named as GPIO 6 on the Banana Pi. Therefore, it is suggested to compare both the pin layouts when using a Raspberry Pi GPIO extension board.

See also

▸ The `readall` parameter is very useful to output pin layout, the names and modes of the pins, and the current values

   $ gpio readall.

▸ The manual page of `gpio` that provides the manual page of the `gpio` command from WiringPi:

   $ man gpio

▸ The *Banana Pro pin definition* forum thread at `http://forum.lemaker.org/thread-10852-1-1-banana_pro_pin_definition.html`. This will give you further information about the Banana Pro pin definition. In the first post, you also find a comparison between Banana Pi, Banana Pro, and Raspberry Pi pin layouts.

Programming the LED

Switching on an LED by a command is one thing. The other is controlling the LED programmatically. In this recipe, we are going to write a real program in C and in Python to switch the LED on and off periodically.

Getting ready

We require the very same breadboard construction from the previous recipe:

▸ A Linux system on the Banana Pi

▸ Access to the shell

▸ A 5 mm LED (forward voltage 2.0 V)

▸ A 470 Ω resistor

▸ A breadboard

▸ Two female to male jumper wires

Construct the circuit as we have seen previously.

How to do it...

Once we have the construction, we can proceed with the steps given in the following sections.

Programming the LED with C

We start by programming the LED in the classic C programming language.

1. Power on your Banana Pi.

2. Open a shell.

3. Create a source code directory and change location to it:

   ```
   $ mkdir ~/source
   $ cd ~/source
   ```

4. Create a source file using nano:

   ```
   $ nano led_test.c
   ```

5. The nano editor will open. Write the following code in C:

   ```c
   #include <wiringPi.h>

   int main(void) {
           // setting up WiringPi and the GPIO 1 pin
           wiringPiSetup();
           pinMode(1, OUTPUT);

           // toggle a HIGH/LOW signal on the GPIO 1 pin
           while (1) {
                   digitalWrite(1, HIGH);
                   delay(1000);
                   digitalWrite(1, LOW);
                   delay(1000);
           }

           return 0;
   }
   ```

In the following screenshot, you see the C code written in the nano editor:

```
  GNU nano 2.2.6              File: led_test.c                      Modified

#include <wiringPi.h>

int main(void) {
        // setting up WiringPi and the GPIO 1 pin
        wiringPiSetup();
        pinMode(1, OUTPUT);

        // toggle a HIGH/LOW signal on the GPIO 1 pin
        while (1) {
                digitalWrite(1, HIGH);
                delay(1000);
                digitalWrite(1, LOW);
                delay(1000);
        }

        return 0;
}

^G Get Help  ^O WriteOut  ^R Read File  ^Y Prev Page  ^K Cut Text   ^C Cur Pos
^X Exit      ^J Justify   ^W Where Is   ^V Next Page  ^U UnCut Text ^T To Spell
```

6. Exit the nano editor and save the changes by pressing *Ctrl + X*, followed by *Y* and *Enter*.

7. Compile the program:

    ```
    $ gcc -Wall -l wiringPi -o led_test led_test.c
    ```

     On some environments, you may need to add some parameters to the GCC command. If the previous compilation did not work for you, try this $ gcc -Wall -lwiringPi -lstdc++ -lpthread -o led_test led_test.c.

8. Run the program with root privileges:

    ```
    $ sudo ./led_test
    ```

    The LED will begin to blink.

9. Abort the program by pressing *Ctrl + C*.

You successfully programmed the LED to toggle it on and off at an interval of one second.

Programming the LED with Python

A lot of applications are programmed in Python these days. We are going to port the previous C code into the Python language:

1. Power on your Banana Pi.

2. Open a shell.

3. Install the required Python packages:

   ```
   $ sudo apt-get install python-dev
   ```

4. Download the GPIO library for Python:

   ```
   $ cd ~
   $ git clone https://github.com/LeMaker/RPi.GPIO_BP -b bananapi
   ```

    If you are using the Banana Pro, use the following command instead:

   ```
   $ git clone https://github.com/LeMaker/
   RPi.GPIO_BP -b bananapro
   ```

5. Change into the downloaded source files directory and build the library:

   ```
   $ cd ~/RPi.GPIO_BP
   $ python setup.py install
   $ sudo python setup.py install
   ```

6. Change to our source directory:

   ```
   $ cd ~/source
   ```

7. Create a source file using nano:

   ```
   $ nano led_test.py
   ```

8. Write the following Python code:

   ```
   import RPi.GPIO as GPIO
   import time

   PIN=12                     # pin 12 is the physical pin of GPIO 1
   GPIO.setmode(GPIO.BOARD)   # setting up GPIO
   GPIO.setup(PIN, GPIO.OUT)  # set GPIO 1 to OUTPUT

   while True:
           GPIO.output(PIN, GPIO.HIGH)
           time.sleep(1)
           GPIO.output(PIN, GPIO.LOW)
           time.sleep(1)
   ```

In the following screenshot, you can see the Python code written in the nano editor:

```
  GNU nano 2.2.6              File: led_test.py                    Modified

import RPi.GPIO as GPIO
import time

PIN=12                    # pin 12 is the physical pin of GPIO 1
GPIO.setmode(GPIO.BOARD)  # setting up GPIO
GPIO.setup(PIN, GPIO.OUT) # set GPIO 1 to OUTPUT

while True:
        GPIO.output(PIN, GPIO.HIGH)
        time.sleep(1)
        GPIO.output(PIN, GPIO.LOW)
        time.sleep(1)

^G Get Help  ^O WriteOut  ^R Read File ^Y Prev Page ^K Cut Text  ^C Cur Pos
^X Exit      ^J Justify   ^W Where Is  ^V Next Page ^U UnCut Text^T To Spell
```

9. Exit the nano editor and save the changes by pressing *Ctrl* + *X*, followed by *Y* and *Enter*.

10. Run the program with root privileges:

```
$ sudo python led_test.py
```

11. Abort the program by pressing *Ctrl* + *C*.

You successfully programmed the LED to toggle it on and off at an interval of one second.

How it works...

You successfully learned to control the LED using C and Python programming languages.

In this recipe, we have two different approaches to access the GPIO 1 pin: the WiringPi approach and the RPi.GPIO approach using the BOARD constant. The `WiringPi` library is used in our C code while the `RPi.GPIO` library is used in our Python code.

The `RPi.GPIO` library addresses the pins by its physical numeration on the Banana Pi board (therefore the BOARD constant). WiringPi identifies the programmable pins mainly by its GPIO numeration. To translate the GPIO number into the physical pin numeration and vice versa, refer to the pin layout tables in the previous recipe.

Both the blocks of code look a bit different, but have the same behavior. Let's take a closer look at the blocks of code.

Explaining the C code

When programming in C, we often require external libraries to make use of additional features. In our case, we are requiring the `WiringPi` library to program the GPIO interface. This is why we are including the WiringPi header file that defines the functions that we need later in the code:

```
#include <wiringPi.h>
```

Every C program starts with the obligatory `main` function:

```
int main(void) {
```

A function has a return type (`int` in our case) and optional parameters (`void` in our case).

All code within the first curly braces (`{` and `}`) is called the body of the function and contains all the code that is executed when the function is executed. The main function is executed once the program itself is executed (therefore, it is called the main function).

The first two lines of the main function are required to set up the WiringPi environment. The `wiringPiSetup()` function initializes WiringPi within our program and the `pinMode(1, OUTPUT)` function sets the GPIO 1 pin to the output mode. Do not forget the semicolon (`;`) at the end of each instruction.

The next instruction starts a so-called infinite loop:

```
while(1) {
```

Just like for a function, all code within the curly braces belong to the `while` loop. This means the next four lines are executed by the `while` loop. It is called an infinite loop, because the loop never ends. The `while` loop loops as long as the condition in the brackets has the status true. In C, the integer (whole number) `1` means the status is true; this is why our `while` loops forever (or at least as long as the program is not aborted).

The next call is `digitalWrite(1, HIGH)`. This instructs to write a logical high signal to the GPIO 1 pin. This switches on the LED. Then we call `delay(1000)`. This lets the program wait for 1000 milliseconds (which is equal to 1 second) until the next instruction is executed. The next two lines are similar, except that this time a logical low signal is written to the GPIO pin, which means we need to switch off the LED. The closing curly braces end the `while` loop.

The last line of the `main` function is `return 0`. As we defined the `main` function to have an integer return type, we are returning 0 at the end of the program. Zero is the exit code for a normal exit of programs.

Explaining the Python code

The Python code behaves exactly like our C program. We require a library to access the GPIO pins (that is, `RPi.GPIO` in our case). As `RPi.GPIO` does not provide a waiting function such as `delay()` in our C program, we also have to import a library that lets our program wait for some time. That is solved by the time library.

Therefore, we are importing the packages `RPi.GPIO` and `time`:

```
import RPi.GPIO as GPIO
import time
```

In Python, we do not need a `main` function necessarily (still we could implement one). Therefore, we start immediately by defining our GPIO 1 pin that is used—`PIN=12`.

Unlike WiringPi that uses the number of the GPIO pin, we need to access the pin by its physical number (that is number 12 in our case). Therefore, we declare the variable PIN with the value `12`. This way, we can just use the PIN variable in the upcoming function calls to refer to the GPIO 1 pin.

The next two lines are initializing the GPIO environment. We want to use the BOARD definition (to access the pin by its physical location):

```
GPIO.setmode(GPIO.BOARD)
```

And we want to set our GPIO pin to the output mode:

```
GPIO.setup(PIN, GPIO.OUT)
```

The next instruction is an infinite while loop:

```
while True:
```

Like in C, we do not have a condition that can be false (as we always use `True`). In Python, we do not use curly braces to define parts of code such as in C. Instead, we are using tabs to indicate that the next four lines belong to the `while` loop.

You probably already assume what the next line does. We just apply a high signal at the GPIO pin, which we referred to by the PIN variable:

```
GPIO.output(PIN, GPIO.HIGH)
```

This will enlighten our LED. To pause our application for 1 second, we use the sleep function of the imported `time` library:

```
time.sleep(1)
```

The next two lines are similar, except that a low signal is written to the GPIO pin meaning to switch off the LED.

Using the GPIO input with a pushbutton

We controlled the LED in the previous two recipes by the GPIO output mode. The next step is to use the GPIO pins as input pins. There is a basic electronic component to demonstrate the GPIO input mode easily—the pushbutton.

In this recipe, we are switching on an LED while a pushbutton is pressed. Once the pushbutton is released, the LED is switched off again.

Getting ready

The following ingredients are required for this recipe:

- A Linux system on the Banana Pi
- Access to the shell
- A 5 mm LED (forward voltage 2.0 V)
- A pushbutton
- A 470 Ω resistor
- A 10K Ω resistor
- A breadboard
- Four female to male jumper wires
- One male to male jumper wire

How to do it...

We build the circuit and program the Banana Pi afterwards.

Preparing the circuit

The circuit in this recipe looks a bit more complex than the previous one.

 Before you connect or disconnect any electrical parts, *power off your Banana Pi* and also *unplug the power supply*.

Let's see how to prepare the circuit:

1. Connect the jumpers, the resistors, the LED, and the pushbutton according the following picture:

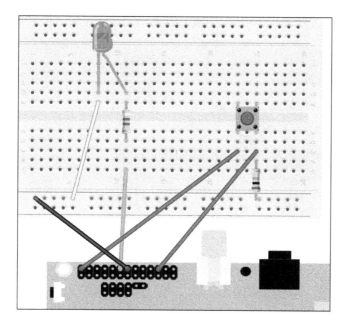

2. Make sure the ground pin (physical pin 14) is connected to the negative (the blue) side of your breadboard.

3. Connect the GPIO 1 pin (physical pin 12) to the same row as you connect your 470 Ω resistor and the anode of the LED.

4. The cathode of the LED is then connected to the negative side of the breadboard via a jumper wire.

5. Connect the 10 kΩ resistor to the negative side of the breadboard and the same row as the pushbutton.

6. Between the pushbutton and the resistor, attach a jumper wire, which is also connected to the GPIO 6 pin (physical pin 22).

7. Finally, connect the other end of the button to the 5.0 V power supply pin (physical pin 2).

Your circuit is completed then.

Programming the software

The final step is to program the software that switches on the LED, once the button is pushed and switches off the LED, once the button is released.

1. Power on your Banana Pi.

2. Open a shell.

3. Change to our previous created source directory:

   ```
   $ cd ~/source
   ```

4. Create a source file using nano:

   ```
   $ nano button_test.c
   ```

5. The nano editor will open. Write the following code in C:

   ```c
   #include <wiringPi.h>

   int main(void) {
       // define constants
       static int const PIN_LED = 1;
       static int const PIN_BUTTON = 6;
       static int const TRUE = 1;

       // setting up WiringPi and the GPIO 1 and 6 pin
       wiringPiSetup();
       pinMode(PIN_LED, OUTPUT);
       pinMode(PIN_BUTTON, INPUT);

       // in this integer, we store the
       // status of the pushbutton
       int buttonStatus;

       // loop forever
       while (TRUE) {
           // read the status of the PIN_BUTTON
           buttonStatus = digitalRead(PIN_BUTTON);

           if (buttonStatus == HIGH) {
               // status of PIN_BUTTON is a HIGH signal
               // switch on the LED
               digitalWrite(PIN_LED, HIGH);
           } else {
               // status of PIN_BUTTON is a LOW signal
   ```

```
                // switch off the LED
                digitalWrite(PIN_LED, LOW);
            }
        }

        return 0;
}
```

The following screenshot shows the C code in the nano editor:

```
  GNU nano 2.2.6                 File: button_test.c

#include <wiringPi.h>

int main(void) {
    // define constants
    static int const PIN_LED = 1;
    static int const PIN_BUTTON = 6;
    static int const TRUE = 1;

    // setting up WiringPi and the GPIO 1 and 6 pin
    wiringPiSetup();
    pinMode(PIN_LED, OUTPUT);
    pinMode(PIN_BUTTON, INPUT);

    // in this integer, we store the status of the pushbutton
    int buttonStatus;

    // loop forever
    while (TRUE) {
        // read the status of the PIN_BUTTON
        buttonStatus = digitalRead(PIN_BUTTON);

        if (buttonStatus == HIGH) {
            // status of PIN_BUTTON is a HIGH signal
            // switch on the LED
            digitalWrite(PIN_LED, HIGH);
        } else {
            // status of PIN_BUTTON is a LOW signal
            // switch off the LED
            digitalWrite(PIN_LED, LOW);
        }
    }

    return 0;
}

^G Get Help   ^O WriteOut   ^R Read File  ^Y Prev Page  ^K Cut Text   ^C Cur Pos
^X Exit       ^J Justify    ^W Where Is   ^V Next Page  ^U UnCut Text ^T To Spell
```

6. Exit the nano editor and save the changes by pressing *Ctrl + X*, followed by *Y* and *Enter*.

7. Compile the program:

```
$ gcc -Wall -l wiringPi -o button_test button_test.c
```

If you get errors, add -lstdc++ -lpthread before –o.

8. Run the program with root privileges:

```
$ sudo ./button_test
```

9. While your program is running, press the button. The LED will be switched on. If you release the button, the LED will switch off again.

The following picture shows the circuit attached to a Banana Pro and the switched on LED while the button is pushed:

10. Abort the program by pressing *Ctrl + C*.

You successfully programmed the LED to toggle it on and off by pushing and releasing the pushbutton as a GPIO input.

How it works...

In this recipe, we make use of a so-called pull-down resistor. It is the 10 kΩ resistor that is connected between the pushbutton and the positive power supply. We require this resistor to define an input state when no signal source is connected. If we had no pull-down resistor, the behavior of the input circuit would depend on factors such as humidity or static energy in the environment. These factors are called noise signals and make our circuit unstable. By using a pull-down resistor, we define a logical low value when the button is not pressed, which avoids the problems with these noise signals.

The pull-down resistor ensures that our program recognizes a logical high signal only if the button is pressed. Otherwise, the program recognizes the defined logical low signal.

Explaining the C code

Just like in the previous recipe, we included the `WiringPi` library. We are also defining the obligatory `main` function. Inside the `main` function, we define three integer constants `PIN_LED` with the value 1, `PIN_BUTTON` with the value 6, and `TRUE` with the value 1. `PIN_LED` and `PIN_BUTTON` are our GPIO pins 1 and 6. You might remember that we have connected the LED to GPIO pin 1 and the pushbutton to GPIO pin 6. The `TRUE` constant is just another constant to increase the readability of the `while` loop condition. Constants are similar to variables and store a value. But unlike variables, the values of the constants cannot be changed after initialization.

Then we are setting up our WiringPi environment by using the `wiringPiSetup()` function and set the mode of pin 1 to `OUTPUT` and of pin 6 to `INPUT`. Instead of writing the pin numbers directly, we are using our previous defined constants. This way, we increased the readability of our code once more.

We declare another integer variable `buttonStatus`. In this variable, we are going to store the current state of the pushbutton. Within our infinite `while` loop, the first instruction is to set the `buttonStatus` variable by reading the GPIO input of our pushbutton. We can read input pins by using the `digitalRead()` function. The `digitalRead()` function requires the pin to read from as a parameter. It returns either a logical high signal (the button is pushed in our case) or a logical low signal (the default state defined by our pull-down resistor, that means released).

To switch on the LED if the button is pressed, we use the `if` statement. The line `if (buttonStatus == HIGH) {` means, if the value of the `buttonStatus` variable is equal to `HIGH` (pushed), then do everything between the curly braces (which is switching on the LED by using `digitalWrite()`). Otherwise, do everything in the curly braces after `else` (which is switching off the LED). When comparing two values if they are equal, it is vital to use the equals sign twice (`buttonStatus == HIGH`). If you write `if (buttonStatus = HIGH)`, the program would work, but not as expected. It will set the `buttonStatus` variable to the value `HIGH`. And as the setting of the variable was successful, the whole statement would be *true*. Therefore, you will always have your LED switched on. So, make sure to use the equals sign *twice* if you want to compare two values.

As in the previous C code, we also need a return value of `0`, which means that everything is okay.

There's more...

Of course you can achieve the same in Python. The Python code looks like:

```
import RPi.GPIO as GPIO

PIN_LED=12                          # pin 12 is the physical pin of GPIO 1
PIN_BUTTON=22                       # pin 22 is the physical pin of GPIO 6

GPIO.setmode(GPIO.BOARD)            # setting up GPIO
GPIO.setup(PIN_LED, GPIO.OUT)       # set GPIO 1 to OUTPUT
GPIO.setup(PIN_BUTTON, GPIO.IN)     # set GPIO 6 to INPUT

while True:
        buttonStatus = GPIO.input(PIN_BUTTON)
        if buttonStatus == GPIO.HIGH:
                GPIO.output(PIN_LED, GPIO.HIGH)
        else:
                GPIO.output(PIN_LED, GPIO.LOW)
```

As you see, the Python code is less extensive but still readable and understandable. It still works exactly like the previous C code. The programming language you need to use when connecting electrical components to your Banana Pi depends on your personal taste.

See also

- ▶ Understanding pull-up and pull-down resistors—a brief introduction into the concept of pull-up and pull-down resistors at `https://makezine.com/2009/03/05/understanding-pullup-and-pulldown-r/`

6
Multimedia

In this chapter, we will cover:

- ▸ Configuring the audio device
- ▸ Getting accelerated video playback
- ▸ Setting up Kodi
- ▸ Setting up an infrared remote control using LIRC

Introduction

Multimedia can be quite challenging on Banana Pi, and a lot of people are frustrated because of advanced low-level problems regarding hardware-accelerated video playback. Therefore, this chapter deals with multimedia-related problems. The two audio outputs (analog and HDMI) are configured. We will discuss and solve the hardware acceleration problem by compiling the important **Video Decode and Presentation API for Unix (VDPAU)** library. Using the previously mentioned components, we are going to configure the video players MPlayer (and its GUI frontend SMPlayer) and VLC. Furthermore, we are going to build Kodi (previously, XBMC) and work around the acceleration problem by using SMPlayer as an external player. Also, we want to introduce the reader to the IR interface, which we are going to configure using the LIRC.

Configuring the audio device

There are two common ways to output audio on Banana Pi. You can pass-through the digital audio signal via HDMI to your television or audio/video receiver, or you can output the signal via the analog line out.

Getting ready

The following ingredients are required to handle audio on Banana Pi:

- A Linux system on Banana Pi
- Access to the shell
- Either an HDMI connection to your TV, audio/video receiver, or...
- A set of stereo headphones or stereo jack cable to any analog audio receiving device with 3.5 mm jack

How to do it...

We are configuring both the HDMI pass-through and the analog audio output in this recipe. In both cases, we have to configure the audio output via the system configuration file `/etc/asound.conf` (also called `asoundrc`).

Configuring HDMI pass-through

The following steps explain how to enable the HDMI pass-through of the digital sound signal:

1. Open a shell.
2. With an editor such as nano, edit or create the system configuration file called `/etc/asound.conf`:

   ```
   $ sudo nano /etc/asound.conf
   ```

3. Enter the following configuration in the file:

   ```
   pcm.!default {
     type hw
     card 1
     device 0
   }
   ctl.!default {
     type hw
     card 1
   }
   ```

The following screenshot shows the nano editor with the `/etc/asound.conf` configuration file to enable HDMI pass-through:

```
  GNU nano 2.2.6                    File: /etc/asound.conf

pcm.!default {
  type hw
  card 1
  device 0
}
ctl.!default {
  type hw
  card 1
}


^G Get Help    ^O WriteOut   ^R Read File  ^Y Prev Page  ^K Cut Text    ^C Cur Pos
^X Exit        ^J Justify    ^W Where Is   ^V Next Page  ^U UnCut Text  ^T To Spell
```

4. Exit and save nano by pressing *Ctrl + X*, followed by *Y* and *Enter*.

5. Reboot your Banana Pi to apply the changes:

```
$ sudo shutdown -r now
```

You have enabled the HDMI pass-through. If you now play an audio or video file, the digital sound stream will be directed to your receiving HDMI device attached to your Banana Pi.

Configuring analog audio

The following steps explain how to enable the output of the sound signal via the analog line out jack:

1. Open a shell.

2. With an editor such as nano, edit or create the system configuration file called `/etc/asound.conf`:

```
$ sudo nano /etc/asound.conf
```

3. Enter the following configuration in the file:

```
pcm.!default {
  type hw
  card 0
  device 0
}
ctl.!default {
  type hw
  card 0
}
```

4. Exit and save nano by pressing *Ctrl + X*, followed by *Y* and *Enter*.

5. Reboot your Banana Pi to apply the changes:

```
$ sudo shutdown -r now
```

You have activated the analog audio output. If you now play an audio or video file, the sound signal will be directed to your headphones or other 3.5 mm stereo jack cable attached to your Banana Pi.

Testing the audio output

To test the audio output, we are going to install a simple audio player, then download and play an open source audio file:

1. Within an opened shell, install the **Sound eXchange** (**SoX**) application and the MP3 decoder for SoX:

```
$ sudo apt-get install sox libsox-fmt-mp3
```

2. Provide or download a test music file, such as the following open source MP3 (*Bring Me Home* by Robert Kunin):

```
$ wget https://archive.org/download/RobertKunin-
BringMeHomeJustTheBlues/RobertKunin-BringMeHome.mp3
```

3. Play the audio file by using the `play` command from SoX:

```
$ play RobertKunin-BringMeHome.mp3
```

4. You should hear the song playing.

5. Abort the `play` command by pressing *Ctrl + C*.

You have just configured your audio output using the ALSA sound system.

How it works...

Linux systems use the **Advanced Linux Sound Architecture** (**ALSA**) system for sound-related tasks. ALSA is the fundamental component of the sound system of Linux computers used to get audio out of sound cards.

The default configuration file of the ALSA system is the `/etc/asound.conf` file (the so-called asoundrc file). This is where we define the system-wide default sound card we are using.

On Banana Pi, you have two sound cards on the board: the analog sound card (number: 0, name: `sunxicodec` or `sunxi-CODEC`) and the HDMI pass-through card (number: 1, name: `sunxisndhdmi` or `sunxi-sndhdmi`).

If we do not have asoundrc configuration, ALSA always uses the first card and its first device (that is the analog audio output) per the default plugin. We can modify the default behavior by creating the system-wide asoundrc file (`/etc/asound.conf`) and superseding the default plugin by declaring a `!default` section for the PCM and the control device. A PCM is the digital audio interface that generates or passes-through the sound signal. The control device (CTL) is used to help the user to control several aspects of the soundcard's behavior.

There's more...

If you are using the analog sound card (`sunxi-CODEC`), you can control the volume via the AlsaMixer on the shell:

```
$ alsamixer
```

As you can see in the following screenshot, a shell frontend is presented where you can adjust the volume level of the output (`Master`) and the input (`Line In`) signal:

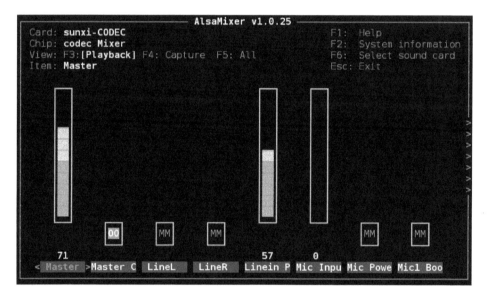

Raise the levels by pressing the up arrow key and lower the levels by pressing the down arrow key. To navigate through the mixer controls, you can also use the left/right arrow keys. You can toggle the muting of various mixers with the *M* key. By pressing *F6*, you can switch between the two sound cards. But keep in mind that the HDMI pass-through has no mixer controls, as you control the volume directly on the receiving device. Quit AlsaMixer by pressing *Esc*.

If you are using PuTTY on Windows, AlsaMixer might look distorted. You can fix it by setting the correct remote character set at **Category | Window | Translation** in the PuTTY settings. Depending on the configuration used, try either UTF-8 or any ISO-8859-1 character set as the remote character set.

If you like to control the ALSA volume levels on the desktop, the Xfce Mixer is recommendable. Install it via Apt by typing:

```
$ sudo apt-get install xfce4-mixer
```

Start the GUI mixer by clicking on the LXDE icon and then navigating to **Sound & Video | Mixer** or by executing the `xfce4-mixer` command.

Select your desired mixer controls by clicking on **Select Controls** and choosing the controls. The following screenshot shows the Xfce Mixer with some activated mixer controls for the analog sound card:

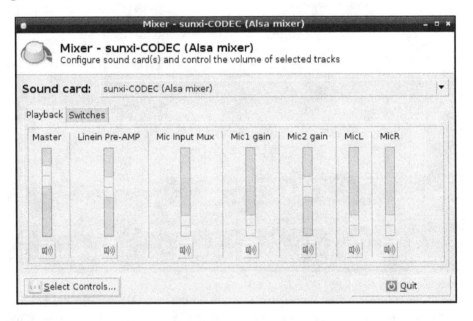

As described in the *How it works...* section, ALSA is a rudimentary yet powerful low-level sound system for Linux. However, if you prefer to have more control or even route the sound signal through your network, you have the possibility to use the sound server PulseAudio in addition to your ALSA system. By using PulseAudio, you also have the opportunity to control the volume level of your HDMI signal, which is not possible using ALSA only. Yet, you should keep in mind that PulseAudio may cause a higher system load. For lack of space, we cannot discuss the configuration of PulseAudio here. However, there are great websites where PulseAudio is described in detail, for example, on the Debian Wiki (see the upcoming *See also* section).

See also

▸ An article about asoundrc configuration on the official ALSA wiki at `http://www.alsa-project.org/main/index.php/Asoundrc`

▸ A library of millions of free books, movies, software, music, and more at `https://archive.org`

▸ The *PulseAudio* article on the Debian wiki at `https://wiki.debian.org/PulseAudio`

Getting accelerated video playback

Many people want to be able to play videos on their Banana Pi in 1080p. Unfortunately, this is quite a complex task, as there are unresolved issues with the software and drivers on Linux. However, it is possible to get accelerated video playback working if you know the required tricks.

In this recipe, we are going to get accelerated video playback working. To do so, we need to perform the following tasks:

1. Build the accelerated Xorg video driver and configure the Xorg server.

2. Build various libraries.

3. Install and configure our video players.

We are going to go through the required tasks step by step.

 This recipe is complex because there are a lot of dependencies and configurations involved. It works on the Raspbian operating system for Banana Pi and Banana Pro. However, on other distributions, the required steps may differ.

Getting ready

The following ingredients are needed to get hardware-accelerated videos working on Banana Pi:

▸ A Linux system on Banana Pi

▸ Access to the shell

▸ An HDMI connection to your TV

▸ A keyboard and mouse connected to your Banana Pi

How to do it...

We are going to prepare our video playback system by building the required components from source. This is necessary to get accelerated video playback and to be able to play 1080p content.

Preparing the building of the required components

As we are going to build several libraries and the `fbturbo` Xorg driver from scratch, we need the source codes and some additional packages at first. Please do the following:

1. Open a shell on your Banana Pi.

2. Create a directory where you want to put all components and change to that directory:

   ```
   $ mkdir ~/video_acceleration
   $ cd ~/video_acceleration
   ```

3. Download all the required source codes: `libdri2`, `libump`, the `sunxi-mali` libraries, the `fbturbo` driver, and `libvdpau-sunxi`, the video-acceleration library:

   ```
   $ git clone https://github.com/robclark/libdri2.git
   $ git clone https://github.com/linux-sunxi/libump.git
   $ git clone https://github.com/linux-sunxi/sunxi-mali.git
   $ git clone https://github.com/ssvb/xf86-video-fbturbo.git
   $ git clone https://github.com/linux-sunxi/libvdpau-sunxi.git
   ```

4. At this point, we should upgrade our system via Apt so that the latest packages are installed:

   ```
   $ sudo apt-get update
   $ sudo apt-get upgrade
   ```

5. Enter Y to continue the system upgrade. This will take some time.

6. Also, we need to install the following packages, as they are required for the upcoming building processes:

   ```
   $ sudo apt-get install libvdpau-dev xorg-dev \
       dh-autoreconf xutils-dev libdrm-dev \
       libegl1-mesa-dev libgles2-mesa-dev
   ```

7. Enter Y to continue the installation of the dependencies.

8. After a few minutes, the required files will be downloaded and installed.

Building and activating the hardware-accelerating components

Depending on the current system load, the building and activation progress of all the components can take some time. To do so, please perform the following steps:

1. Build and install the `libdri2` library:

    ```
    $ cd ~/video_acceleration/libdri2
    $ ./autogen.sh --prefix=/usr
    $ sudo make install
    ```

2. Build and install the `libump` library:

    ```
    $ cd ~/video_acceleration/libump
    $ autoreconf -vi
    $ ./configure --prefix=/usr
    $ make
    $ sudo make install
    ```

3. Build and install the `sunxi-mali` libraries:

    ```
    $ cd ~/video_acceleration/sunxi-mali
    $ git submodule init
    $ git submodule update
    $ sudo mkdir /usr/lib/mali
    $ make config ABI=armhf VERSION=r3p0
    $ sudo make -C include install
    $ sudo make -C lib/mali prefix=/usr/ libdir='/usr/lib/mali/'
    install
    ```

4. Create a `/etc/ld.so.conf.d/1-mali.conf` file as root to tell the system to use the Mali libraries we have built:

    ```
    $ sudo -s
    # echo "/usr/lib/mali" > /etc/ld.so.conf.d/1-mali.conf
    # ldconfig
    # exit
    ```

5. Now, build and install the `fbturbo` Xorg driver:

    ```
    $ cd ~/video_acceleration/xf86-video-fbturbo
    $ autoreconf -vi
    $ ./configure --prefix=/usr
    $ make
    $ sudo make install
    ```

6. To tell the system to use our new built `fbturbo` Xorg driver, create a Xorg configuration file:

    ```
    $ sudo nano /etc/X11/xorg.conf
    ```

7. The nano editor will open. Enter the following Xorg configuration that you can also find on the Packt Publishing website to copy and paste easily:

```
Section "Screen"
        Identifier      "My Screen"
        Device          "Allwinner A10/A13 FBDEV"
        Monitor         "My Monitor"
EndSection

Section "Device"
        Identifier      "Allwinner A10/A13 FBDEV"
        Driver          "fbturbo"
        Option          "fbdev" "/dev/fb0"
        Option          "SwapbuffersWait" "true"
        Option          "AccelMethod" "G2D"
EndSection

Section "Monitor"
        Identifier      "My Monitor"
        Option          "DPMS" "false"
EndSection
```

The following screenshot shows the nano editor with the required Xorg configuration:

```
  GNU nano 2.2.6            File: /etc/X11/xorg.conf              Modified

Section "Screen"
        Identifier      "My Screen"
        Device          "Allwinner A10/A13 FBDEV"
        Monitor         "My Monitor"
EndSection

Section "Device"
        Identifier      "Allwinner A10/A13 FBDEV"
        Driver          "fbturbo"
        Option          "fbdev" "/dev/fb0"
        Option          "SwapbuffersWait" "true"
        Option          "AccelMethod" "G2D"
EndSection

Section "Monitor"
        Identifier      "My Monitor"
        Option          "DPMS" "false"
EndSection

^G Get Help    ^O WriteOut    ^R Read File   ^Y Prev Page   ^K Cut Text    ^C Cur Pos
^X Exit        ^J Justify     ^W Where Is    ^V Next Page   ^U UnCut Text  ^T To Spell
```

8. Exit and save nano by pressing *Ctrl + X*, followed by *Y* and *Enter*.

9. To get the Mali subsystem working, we also need to instruct the system to assign the correct permissions for certain device files on boot. To do so, create a `udev` rule:

```
$ sudo nano /etc/udev/rules.d/50-mali.rules
```

10. Enter the following `udev` rules, which you will also find on the Packt Publishing website, into the opened editor:

```
KERNEL=="mali", MODE="0660", GROUP="video"
KERNEL=="ump", MODE="0660", GROUP="video"
KERNEL=="disp", MODE="0660", GROUP="video"
KERNEL=="g2d", MODE="0660", GROUP="video"
KERNEL=="fb*", MODE="0660", GROUP="video"
KERNEL=="cedar_dev", MODE="0660", GROUP="video"
```

The following screenshot shows the nano editor with the entered `udev` rules:

11. Exit and save nano by pressing *Ctrl + X*, followed by *Y* and *Enter*.

12. Build and install the `libvdpau` library:

```
$ cd ~/video_acceleration/libvdpau-sunxi
$ make
$ sudo make install
```

13. We have to create a persistent environment variable to tell the system that there is a VDPAU driver. To do so, add the line `export VDPAU_DRIVER=sunxi` in the `/etc/profile` configuration file with root privileges:

```
$ sudo -s
# echo "export VDPAU_DRIVER=sunxi" >> /etc/profile
# exit
```

14. Reboot Banana Pi to apply all the previous modifications:

```
$ sudo shutdown -r now
```

15. Once Banana Pi is rebooted, you can check if the environment variable is set correctly. Open another shell and type the following:

```
$ echo $VDPAU_DRIVER
```

16. The shell should respond with sunxi.

17. As an optional step, we can now test our hardware acceleration by compiling and running a test application provided by Sunxi Mali. On the desktop, please continue with the following steps.

18. Within your terminal, change to the test directory of the Mali source code directory:

```
$ cd ~/video_acceleration/sunxi-mali/test
```

19. Compile the test application:

```
$ cc -Wall -o test test.c -lEGL -lGLESv2 -lX11
```

20. Run the test application within a terminal on your desktop:

```
$ ./test
```

The following screenshot shows the successful Sunxi Mali hardware acceleration test:

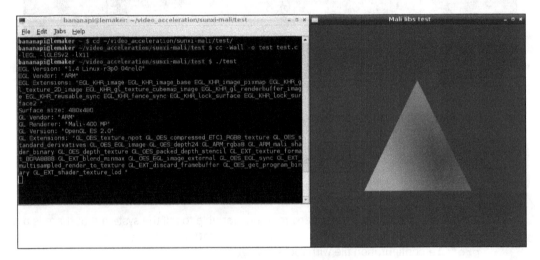

The VDPAU driver is now installed successfully. We can continue by installing our media players.

Installing and configuring MPlayer

MPlayer is a versatile movie player that runs on a lot of systems. It supports nearly all types of audio and video files. We are going to install MPlayer itself and the GUI frontend SMPlayer:

1. Within a shell, install the mplayer2 and smplayer packages:

```
$ sudo apt-get install mplayer2 smplayer
```

To pretty up the SMPlayer frontend later, you can also install the optional package: `smplayer-themes`.

2. Enter Y to continue the installation of the dependency packages.

3. We will download the open source movie *Sintel* to test the hardware-accelerated video playback:

```
$ wget http://ftp.nluug.nl/pub/graphics/blender/
demo/movies/Sintel.2010.1080p.mkv
```

The download will take some time since the file size is around 1.1 GB.

4. When the download is finished, switch to your desktop and open the LXTerminal application.

5. Within the terminal, start MPlayer with the correct parameters for VDPAU video output and the VDPAU video codecs:

```
$ mplayer -vo vdpau -vc ffmpeg12vdpau,ffh264vdpau,
Sintel.2010.1080p.mkv
```

The following screenshot shows the hardware-accelerated MPlayer playing the Sintel movie:

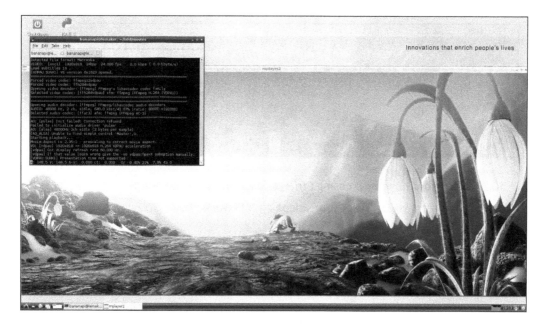

6. The following line is outputted by MPlayer on the terminal indicating that the video is hardware accelerated: `Selected video codec: [ffh264vdpau] vfm: ffmpeg (FFmpeg H.264 (VDPAU))`.

7. Once the hardware acceleration test is successful, you can quit the MPlayer, for example, by pressing the *Q* key.

8. To persist the use of VDPAU per default, we add the `~/.mplayer/config` configuration file:

   $ nano ~/.mplayer/config

9. The nano editor will open; add the following lines:

   ```
   vo=vdpau
   vc=ffmpeg12vdpau,ffh264vdpau,
   fullscreen=yes
   quiet=yes
   ao=alsa
   ```

 If you are using another sound system such as PulseAudio, please replace `ao=alsa` with `ao=pulse` or the appropriate name. See *audio output drivers* in the manual page of mplayer (`$ man mplayer`).

The following screenshot shows the MPlayer configuration in the nano editor:

10. Exit and save nano by pressing *Ctrl + X*, followed by *Y* and *Enter*.

    From now on, you can play your videos on MPlayer without explicitly using the `-vc` and `-vo` parameters.

11. Now, we will set up SMPlayer as a convenient GUI frontend for MPlayer. Run the previously installed SMPlayer by clicking on the LXDE icon and then navigating to **Sound & Video | SMPlayer**. Or, simply start it by executing `smplayer` in a terminal application.

12. When SMPlayer opens, click on **Options | Preferences** in the menu (or press *Ctrl + P*).

13. Verify that the text field **MPlayer executable** has the value `mplayer`.

14. Change to the **Video** tab and check that **vdpau** is selected as the output driver.

15. Within the **Audio** tab, choose **alsa** as the audio driver. Depending on your desired sound system, you may choose a different audio driver.

16. Save the changes by clicking on **OK**.

17. Click on **Open** | **File** (or press *Ctrl* + *F*) , which will show the file-choosing dialog and open the test movie.

18. The video should start immediately in SMPlayer.

Congratulations! You have managed to install a hardware-accelerated video player onto your Banana Pi.

Installing and configuring VLC media player

If you prefer VLC media player, you can install it as well.

Unfortunately, the VLC package provided by Apt is not completely compatible with the VDPAU solution we have just set up. Therefore, we are forced to build VLC from source. To build the VLC version 2.2, we require some current packages that are unfortunately not provided by the Debian 7 (*Wheezy*, used by Raspbian) repository. Therefore, we are also forced to acquire some packages from the latest Debian 8 (*Jessie*) repository.

 The addition of another release version of Debian can be risky. You could break version dependencies on your current setup easily. Please follow the next steps carefully.

Furthermore, you will need to have a lot of free space to build VLC media player. It is recommended that you use an SD card of 16 GB or more or to build the source code on an external HDD/SSD.

1. Within your opened shell, install the following packages:

```
$ sudo apt-get install gcc-4.8 lua5.2 liblua5.2-dev \
    libmad0-dev liba52-0.7.4-dev libxcb-shm0-dev \
    libxcb-composite0-dev libxcb-xv0-dev libqt4-dev \
    libxcb-randr0-dev libasound2-dev libgcrypt11-dev
```

2. Enter Y to continue the installation of the dependencies.

3. Edit the `/etc/apt/sources.list` file to add the `jessie` repository:

```
$ sudo nano /etc/apt/sources.list
```

4. Add the following line to the existing repository source:

```
deb http://mirrordirector.raspbian.org/raspbian/ jessie
main contrib non-free
```

The following screenshot shows the opened `sources.list` file on the nano editor with the default `wheezy` repository and the added `jessie` repository:

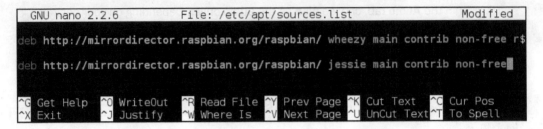

5. Exit and save nano by pressing *Ctrl + X*, followed by *Y* and *Enter*.

6. Also create `/etc/apt/preferences` file to define the priorities of the two competing repositories:

```
$ sudo nano /etc/apt/preferences
```

7. Add the following configuration to prioritize the current `wheezy` repository over the new `jessie` repository:

```
Package: *
Pin: release n=wheezy
Pin-Priority: 900

Package: *
Pin: release n=jessie
Pin-Priority: 100
```

The following screenshot shows the complete Apt preferences configuration within the nano editor:

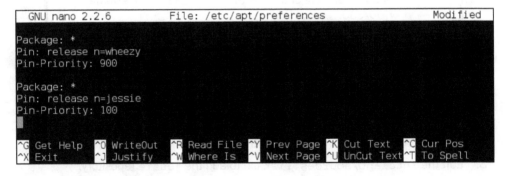

8. Exit and save nano by pressing *Ctrl + X*, followed by *Y* and *Enter*.

9. With the new repository added, we will now install the required dependency packages explicit from the `jessie` repository after updating the Apt cache:

```
$ sudo apt-get update
```

```
$ sudo apt-get -t jessie install libavformat-dev \
    libswscale-dev libvdpau-dev
```

10. Enter Y to continue the installation of the dependencies.

11. While Apt is installing the dependency packages, you will be asked if you want to restart services. Confirm restarting by entering Yes.

12. Once the configuration of the new packages is done, download the source code of VLC from their Git repository:

```
$ git clone git://git.videolan.org/vlc/vlc-2.2.git
```

13. Change the current location to the downloaded source code directory:

```
$ cd vlc-2.2
```

14. Start the bootstrap shell script to prepare the upcoming building process:

```
$ ./bootstrap
```

15. Export the C compiler and Lua compiler environment variables, and start the configuration script with the following arguments:

```
$ export CC=gcc-4.8
$ export LUAC=/usr/bin/luac5.2
$ ./configure --prefix=/usr --sysconfdir=/etc
```

16. Initiate the building and installation process:

```
$ make
$ sudo make install
```

17. The building and installation of VLC media player will take some time. Once this process is finished, we can finally start VLC.

18. If necessary, switch to your Banana Pi desktop and start VLC by executing the vlc command in a terminal on your desktop:

```
$ vlc
```

19. When VLC starts, navigate to the preferences by selecting **Tools | Preferences** from the main menu or pressing *Ctrl + P*.

    The **Preferences** dialog will open.

20. Make sure that the **Simple** radio box is checked on the bottom-right corner.

21. Navigate to **Input & Codecs** via the upper options and select the VDPAU video decoder value for **Hardware-accelerated decoding**.

22. Save the settings by clicking on **Save**.

You have installed VLC media player including VDPAU hardware acceleration on your Banana Pi successfully.

How it works...

In this recipe, we did a lot of advanced things. We built various libraries and drivers directly from the source code and configuring media players. But why is it so complicated to get accelerated video playback? The reasons are versatile. In fact, the graphical unit (the Mali GPU) of Banana Pi is designed originally for mobile devices. Perfect drivers are available for the Android system only. Therefore, the Mali GPU is not 100 percent supported out of the box on single-board computers running Linux—like our Banana Pi.

However, we managed to get the hardware acceleration working and play 1080p video files by using the VDPAU library we just built.

When we built the Mali libraries, we created a `/etc/ld.so.conf.d/1-mali.conf` file with the content `/usr/lib/mali`. Configuration files under `/etc/ld.so.conf.d` are used to give the system an alternative to where libraries could be located. In our case, we installed the compiled Mali libraries into the optional directory `/usr/lib/mali` because the Raspbian distribution also provides libraries with the same names (for example, `libEGL.so`), which we should not delete. Since we named the configuration file `1-mali.conf`, it has the alphabetical highest priority. The system will use our built `libEGL.so`, `libGLESv2.so`, and so forth when a program needs to access these libraries instead of the pre-shipped libraries under `/usr/lib/arm-linux-gnueabihf/`.

We have also built the Xorg driver `fbturbo`. The Xorg server draws the whole graphical user interface (that is your desktop and the graphical applications) on your display. To the `fbturbo` driver, we have to provide a Xorg configuration (`/etc/X11/xorg.conf`) that instructs the Xorg server to use the `fbturbo` driver.

The libraries and drivers access essential hardware components of our Banana Pi, such as the frame buffer. These hardware components are accessible by device files such as `/dev/fb0`. To allow the user to access these hardware components, we have to assign read and write permissions for these device files.

We automatically assign these permissions on boot using the `udev` system by creating a `udev` rule (`/etc/udev/rules.d/50-mali.rules`). The device manager `udev` is responsible for various hardware-related tasks on your Linux system. By providing our Mali rule, the `udev` system can automatically assign permissions. Our `udev` rule tells `udev` to assign `660` (`rw-rw----`) permissions for the device files `/dev/ump`, `/dev/mali`, and so on. It also instructs `udev` to change the group of these device files to the `video` group. Since the default Banana Pi user (`bananapi`) is a member of the `video` group, he/she then has read and write access to these files. If you are using another user, please ensure your user is member of the `video` group (see the *User maintenance* recipe in *Chapter 2, Administration*).

We also built the VDPAU library (`libvdpau_sunxi`). VDPAU is a standardized interface to allow software such as media players to access the hardware acceleration. This is done via a library implementing the VDPAU interface (`libvdpau`). To tell the system which VDPAU implementing library has to be used, an environment variable (`VDPAU_DRIVER`) has to be set. Environment variables are shell variables that are valid everywhere on the system, not only in a single shell script. You can create an environment variable using the `export` command. To persist our `VDPAU_DRIVER` variable with the value `sunxi` (meaning to use the `libvdpau_sunxi` library), we add the `export` command in the `/etc/profile` file. The `/etc/profile` file is loaded on every system boot. As we did not execute the `export` command directly in this recipe, the `VDPAU_DRIVER` variable is available after the next reboot (that is, when the `/etc/profile` is reloaded).

Once all the required libraries and drivers are built, we can use MPlayer to play videos with high-definition resolutions using hardware-accelerated VDPAU library. To do so, we have to tell MPlayer to use the VDPAU video output (`-vo vdpau`) and the VDPAU-compatible video codecs (`-vc ffmpeg12vdpau,ffh264vdpau,`). To avoid using these MPlayer parameters on each start, we persist these settings in the `~/.mplayer/config` file.

The graphical frontend SMPlayer offers a convenient way to integrate MPlayer into your desktop environment. As the name implies, it uses MPlayer as its main component but builds a decent graphical interface around it.

Unfortunately, we cannot install VLC media player from Apt like we did with MPlayer. The VLC media player that is provided by the Raspbian repository is compiled for the Raspberry Pi and, therefore, is not 100 percent compatible with the hardware acceleration on Banana Pi. This is why we compiled VLC media player from source code in this recipe.

Version 2.2 of VLC is able to use the hardware acceleration via VPDAU. To build version 2.2, we were forced to acquire packages that are not on Wheezy, the default repository of Debian 7, used by Raspbian. Therefore, we added the newer Debian 8 `jessie` repository to Apt's `sources.list` to be able to get the newer packages we need. As we do not want to upgrade our whole system to possibly break anything by Debian `jessie`, we also need to lower the priority of the added Jessie repository. This is done by a mechanism called **Apt Pinning** in the `/etc/apt/preferences` file. After doing so, we can update the Apt cache to make the `jessie` repository available and install the packages we need from the repository explicitly.

After cloning the source code of VLC 2.2, we initiated the bootstrap script to prepare the configure script. We also need to compile VLC and its components with the newer GCC 4.8 compiler (instead of the default 4.6 version). This is why we define GCC 4.8 as our C compiler by exporting the CC environment variable. Then we finally can initiate the triad of `configure`, `make`, and `make install`.

There's more...

When building and installing applications using the `make` command, you do not have the possibility of package managers such as Apt. You cannot update the application easily, nor have you the possibility of automatic dependency management. Please keep in mind that if you update, for example, your Xorg server, you could break the compatibility with your compiled `fbturbo` driver. In this case, you may need to log in to your Banana Pi using SSH and rebuild the `fbturbo` driver.

To uninstall self-built applications or libraries, you can also use the `make` command:

```
$ sudo make uninstall
```

See also

- ▶ How to build the Mali driver on linux-sunxi.org at `https://linux-sunxi.org/Mali_binary_driver`
- ▶ The documentation of the Xorg configuration at `http://www.x.org/archive/X11R7.7/doc/man/man5/xorg.conf.5.xhtml`
- ▶ The Wikipedia article about the udev device manager at `https://en.wikipedia.org/wiki/Udev`
- ▶ The *AptPreferences* article that explains the mechanism of Apt-Pinning at `https://wiki.debian.org/AptPreferences`
- ▶ The *Durian Open Movie* project at `https://durian.blender.org/about/`

Setting up Kodi

Another often-desired use case for Banana Pi is a media center. Kodi—formerly known as **XBMC**—and is the de facto standard for media centers. Therefore, people want to get Kodi on their devices.

The bad news is that to date, for several reasons, it is not possible to get hardware-accelerated video playback within the default player of Kodi on Banana Pi. It is also meaningless to just install the Kodi package from the Raspbian repository as it is compiled for the Raspberry Pi (just like VLC). Therefore, it does not work on the Banana Pi hardware.

However, we can compile Kodi from source and configure an external player to play 1080p content. Like in the previous recipe, this is also quite a complex and time-consuming task.

In this recipe, we are going to build a Kodi setup with working accelerated video playback by an external video player. To do this, it is necessary that you have configured at least one working hardware-accelerated video player (MPlayer or VLC) from the previous recipe.

Getting ready

The following ingredients are required to get Kodi working on Banana Pi:

- A Linux system on Banana Pi
- Access to the shell
- An HDMI connection to your TV
- A keyboard and mouse connected to your Banana Pi
- A configured video player with hardware acceleration (see the previous recipe, *Getting accelerated video playback*)

How to do it...

The building of Kodi itself is relatively simple if you have completed the steps of the previous recipe. Let's do it:

 Just like in the previous recipe, you will need to have a lot of free space to build the Kodi media center.

1. Open a shell on your Banana Pi.
2. You will need to install a lot of new packages to be able to build Kodi. To copy and paste the following packages, you can go to the Packt Publishing website or the *Compile Kodi for Linux* link mentioned in the *See also* section of this recipe.

   Install the following packages:

```
$ sudo apt-get install automake autopoint bison \
    build-essential ccache cmake curl cvs default-jre \
    gawk gdc gettext git-core gperf libasound2-dev \
    libass-dev libavcodec-dev libavfilter-dev \
    libavformat-dev libavutil-dev libbluetooth-dev \
    libbluray-dev libbluray1 libboost-dev \
    libboost-thread-dev libbz2-dev libcap-dev \
    libcdio-dev libcec-dev libcec1 libcurl3 \
    libcurl4-gnutls-dev libcwiid-dev libcwiid1 \
    libdbus-1-dev libenca-dev libflac-dev \
    libfontconfig-dev libfreetype6-dev libfribidi-dev \
    libglew-dev libiso9660-dev libjasper-dev \
    libjpeg-dev libltdl-dev liblzo2-dev libmad0-dev \
    libmicrohttpd-dev libmodplug-dev libmp3lame-dev \
    libmpeg2-4-dev libmpeg3-dev libmysqlclient-dev \
    libnfs-dev libogg-dev libpcre3-dev libplist-dev \
```

```
libpng-dev libpostproc-dev libpulse-dev \
libsamplerate-dev libsdl-dev libsdl-gfx1.2-dev \
libsdl-image1.2-dev libsdl-mixer1.2-dev \
libshairport-dev libsmbclient-dev libsqlite3-dev \
libssh-dev libssl-dev libswscale-dev libtiff-dev \
libtinyxml-dev libtool libudev-dev libusb-dev \
libva-dev libva-egl1 libva-tpi1 libvdpau-dev \
libvorbisenc2 libxml2-dev libxmu-dev libxrandr-dev \
libxrender-dev libxslt1-dev libxt-dev libyajl-dev \
mesa-utils nasm pmount python-dev python-imaging \
python-sqlite swig unzip yasm zip zlib1g-dev gcc-4.8 \
libtag1-dev
```

3. Enter Y to continue the installation of the dependencies.

4. When the packages are installed, you can download the source code of Kodi:

   ```
   $ git clone -b Helix https://github.com/xbmc/xbmc.git
   ```

5. Change to the downloaded source directory:

   ```
   $ cd xbmc
   ```

6. Start the bootstrap script:

   ```
   $ ./bootstrap
   ```

7. Export the following environment variables:

   ```
   $ export CC=gcc-4.8
   ```

   ```
   $ export CFLAGS='-march=armv7-a -mfloat-abi=hard'
   ```

8. Initiate the configuration script:

   ```
   $ ./configure --disable-debug --disable-vdpau --disable-vaapi
   ```

   While configuring, various essential components for Kodi are built from source. The configuration will take up to one hour to complete.

9. Build and install Kodi:

   ```
   $ make
   ```

   The building process of Kodi takes a lot of time (a few hours). Eventually the shell will output the following message:

   ```
   -----------------------
   Kodi built successfully
   -----------------------
   ```

10. Finally, you are ready to install Kodi:

    ```
    $ sudo make install
    ```

Once Kodi is installed successfully, we can configure Kodi to use a video player as an external player.

11. Edit or create a `playercorefactory.xml` file within your Kodi configuration directory:

```
$ nano ~/.kodi/userdata/playercorefactory.xml
```

12. Add the following external player configuration to let Kodi open MKV files with SMPlayer:

```
<playercorefactory>
 <players>
   <player name="smplayer" type="ExternalPlayer" audio="true" video="true">
     <filename>/usr/bin/smplayer</filename>
     <args>-minigui -close-at-end -fullscreen "{1}"</args>
     <hidexbmc>false</hidexbmc>
   </player>
 </players>
 <rules action="prepend">
   <rule filetypes="mkv" filename="*.*" player="smplayer"/>
 </rules>
</playercorefactory>
```

The following screenshot shows the external player configuration of Kodi within the nano editor:

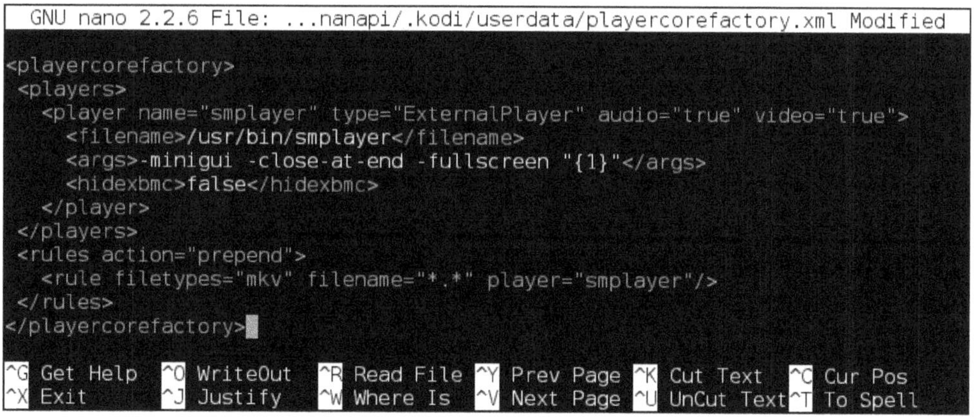

13. Exit and save nano by pressing *Ctrl + X*, followed by *Y* and *Enter*.

14. If necessary, switch to your desktop and open the LXTerminal application.

15. Within the terminal, start the Kodi media center:

```
$ kodi
```

The following screenshot shows the Kodi logo while loading the media center on Banana Pi:

16. When Kodi is started for the first time, it will update some components from the Internet. After a few seconds or minutes, it will be ready to use.

17. Navigate to **Videos** | **Files** | **Add Videos...** | **Browse** and choose a directory containing video files (for example, the Sintel movie).

18. Close the dialogs by clicking on **OK**. The directory containing the video files will be added to the video library.

19. Enter the added video directory and play a movie file.

20. If the video is an MKV file, Kodi will open the hardware-accelerated SMPlayer and let it play the MKV file.

You have successfully installed Kodi on Banana Pi and configured an external player to bypass the hardware acceleration problem.

How it works...

Just like in the previous recipe, we build the Kodi media center from the source code. As Kodi has a huge number of features, it requires a lot of packages pre-installed before we can build it along with its components.

Once these dependency packages are installed, we are ready to clone the source codes and initiate the building. The bootstrap script sets up the upcoming configuration script. The configuration script makes sure that all the required dependencies are met and begins the building of helper components that are needed for Kodi (for example, the multimedia solution FFmpeg). The building of Kodi itself is a time-consuming task on Banana Pi, since it is such a comprehensive media center solution.

Unfortunately, to date, it is not possible to use the internal player of Kodi for hardware-accelerated video playback on Banana Pi. The chances that this will be solved in the future are good, but until then, we need to work around the problem. Luckily, Kodi offers the concept of external players. By using an external player that is configured in the playercorefactory.xml file, we instruct Kodi to open specific multimedia files with external programs. In our case, we make use of SMPlayer we built in the previous recipe to play 1080p videos hardware accelerated while still having the functionalities of Kodi.

Consequently, the interface of the SMPlayer is not really integrated into Kodi. This means that you cannot use the features of Kodi while playing videos via SMPlayer. In my opinion however, the method used in this recipe offers the best possible solution to get a stable media center experience on Banana Pi.

There's more...

If you prefer to run your Banana Pi as a media center only, you may start Kodi automatically after booting your device.

To start Kodi on boot, do the following:

1. Open a shell on your Banana Pi.

2. Create the `~/.config/lxsession/LXDE` directories if not existent:

   $ mkdir -p ~/.config/lxsession/LXDE

3. Create or edit the `~/.config/lxsession/LXDE/autostart` file:

   $ nano ~/.config/lxsession/LXDE/autostart

4. Add the following line:

   `@kodi-standalone`

5. Exit and save nano by pressing *Ctrl + X*, followed by *Y* and *Enter*.

6. Reboot Banana Pi to test the autostart of Kodi on boot:

```
$ sudo shutdown -r now
```

Kodi should start automatically on boot from now on. To disable Kodi on boot, simply remove the @kodi-standalone line in the autostart file or delete that file.

See also

▸ The compilation guide for Linux on the official Kodi wiki at
  http://kodi.wiki/view/HOW-TO:Compile_Kodi_for_Linux

▸ The wiki article on how to configure the playercorefactory.xml file at
  http://kodi.wiki/view/External_players

▸ The Wikipedia article about the multimedia solution FFmpeg at
  https://en.wikipedia.org/wiki/FFmpeg

Setting up an infrared remote control using LIRC

In the last recipe of this book, we will discover the possibilities of setting up an infrared remote control using the LIRC application.

Getting ready

The following components are needed to set up a remote control on Banana Pi:

▸ A Linux system on Banana Pi

▸ A remote control sending infrared signals

▸ An HDMI connection to your TV

▸ A keyboard and mouse connected to your Banana Pi

This recipe is valid for most remote controls. We are using a remote control (shown in the following picture) of a well-known manufacturer:

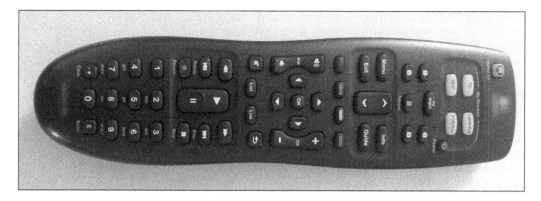

In most cases, any other remote control should work just fine if it emits infrared signals.

How to do it...

As a first step, we need to set up LIRC to recognize each button pressed on your remote control. Afterwards, we need to configure what should happen when we press buttons on the remote control.

Configuring LIRC to recognize the remote control

The following steps explain how to set up a remote control with LIRC:

1. Boot your Banana Pi into the desktop.

2. Open the LXTerminal application.

3. Install the following packages:

   ```
   $ sudo apt-get install lirc lirc-x xinput evtest
   ```

4. Enter Y to confirm the installation of the dependency packages.

5. Once the packages are installed, disable the default `sunxi-ir` device:

   ```
   $ xinput disable sunxi-ir
   ```

6. To persist the disabling of the `sunxi-ir` device, execute the previous command when the LXDE desktop loads.

7. Create the `~/.config/lxsession/LXDE` directories if not existent:

   ```
   $ mkdir -p ~/.config/lxsession/LXDE
   ```

8. Create or edit the `~/.config/lxsession/LXDE/autostart` file:

   ```
   $ nano ~/.config/lxsession/LXDE/autostart
   ```

9. Add the following line:

   ```
   @xinput disable sunxi-ir
   ```

10. Exit and save nano by pressing *Ctrl + X*, followed by *Y* and *Enter*.

11. Type the following command to determine the correct event device:

    ```
    $ cat /proc/bus/input/devices | grep -A 10 sunxi-ir | grep event
    ```

12. The shell will respond with something like `H: Handlers=sysrq rfkill kbd event0`. This tells you that in the previous case, the correct device file is `/dev/input/event0`.

13. Test whether the remote control works with Banana Pi by running the `evtest` command:

    ```
    $ evtest /dev/input/event0
    ```

    Replace `/dev/input/event0` with your correct event device if necessary.

14. Press some buttons on your remote control.

15. If the `evtest` command recognizes the key presses, it shows something like this:

    ```
    Event: … (EV_KEY), code 104 (KEY_PAGEUP), value 1
    Event: … -------------- SYN_REPORT ------------
    Event: … (EV_KEY), code 104 (KEY_PAGEUP), value 0
    Event: … -------------- SYN_REPORT ------------
    ```

    In this case, the remote works like a charm. If you did not get a similar output, the remote control is potentially incompatible with your Banana Pi.

16. Quit the `evtest` program by pressing *Ctrl + C*.

17. Now we need to configure LIRC. Edit the `/etc/lirc/hardware.conf` file with an editor like nano:

    ```
    $ sudo nano /etc/lirc/hardware.conf
    ```

18. You will find a handful of configuration options within that file. Set the `DRIVER` variable to `devinput` and the `DEVICE` variable to the event device file:

    ```
    DRIVER="devinput"
    DEVICE="/dev/input/event0"
    ```

The following screenshot shows the correct configured DRIVER and DEVICE option:

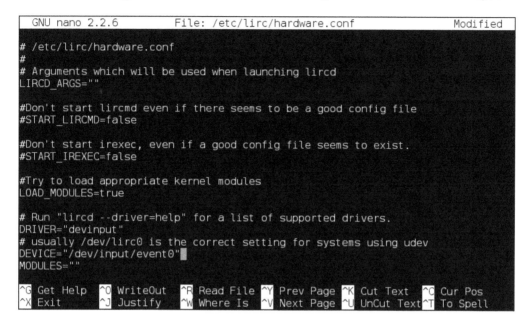

```
  GNU nano 2.2.6          File: /etc/lirc/hardware.conf          Modified

# /etc/lirc/hardware.conf
#
# Arguments which will be used when launching lircd
LIRCD_ARGS=""

#Don't start lircmd even if there seems to be a good config file
#START_LIRCMD=false

#Don't start irexec, even if a good config file seems to exist.
#START_IREXEC=false

#Try to load appropriate kernel modules
LOAD_MODULES=true

# Run "lircd --driver=help" for a list of supported drivers.
DRIVER="devinput"
# usually /dev/lirc0 is the correct setting for systems using udev
DEVICE="/dev/input/event0"
MODULES=""

^G Get Help  ^O WriteOut  ^R Read File ^Y Prev Page ^K Cut Text  ^C Cur Pos
^X Exit      ^J Justify   ^W Where Is  ^V Next Page ^U UnCut Text^T To Spell
```

19. Exit and save nano by pressing *Ctrl + X*, followed by *Y* and *Enter*.

20. Copy a generic remote control configuration file to `/etc/lirc/lircd`:

    ```
    $ sudo cp /usr/share/lirc/remotes/generic/NEC.conf
    /etc/lirc/lircd
    ```

21. To configure the buttons of the remote control, we need the button names used by LIRC. To get a list of all button names, it is recommended to run the following command in another shell:

    ```
    $ irrecord --list-names
    ```

22. Start configuring the buttons of your remote control:

    ```
    $ sudo irrecord -H devinput -d /dev/input/event0
    /etc/lirc/lircd
    ```

23. The `irrecord` application will output some introducing words. Continue by pressing *Enter*.

24. Add a key by entering the name of the key (which you determined using `irrecord --list-names`). For example, `KEY_0`:

    ```
    Please enter the name for the next button (press <ENTER> to finish
    recording)
    KEY_0
    ```

25. The `irrecord` application will respond with `Now hold down button "KEY_0"`.

26. Press and hold the appropriate button on your remote control (the button 0 in our example) until `irrecord` recognizes the key press.

27. Repeat the previous procedure until you have configured all the keys you need.

28. When you are finished configuring your remote control buttons, press *Enter* to quit the `irrecord` configuration.

29. The configuration tool will create the actual LIRD configuration (`/etc/lirc/lircd.conf`) and respond with the following:

```
irrecord: closing '/dev/input/event0'
irrecord: initializing '/dev/input/event0'
irrecord: closing '/dev/input/event0'
Successfully written config file.
```

30. Check your `/etc/lirc/lircd.conf` using an editor such as nano:

```
$ sudo nano /etc/lirc/lircd.conf
```

31. Scroll down until you see your configured button names. If you see more than one hex code per line, delete the second hex code. In the following screenshot, you see that `KEY_0` and `KEY_ENTER` are still misconfigured. The remaining visible buttons are configured correctly.

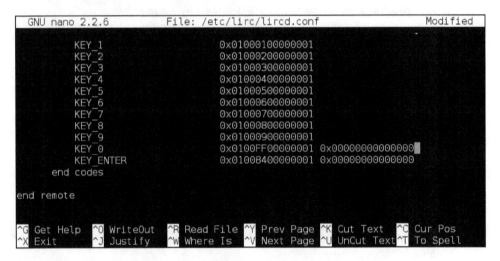

32. Exit and save nano by pressing *Ctrl + X*, followed by *Y* and *Enter*.

33. Restart the LIRC service:

```
$ sudo /etc/init.d/lirc restart
```

34. Test your LIRC configuration using the irw tool:

```
$ irw
```

35. Press some of the configured buttons on your remote control. The irw tool will output something like the following:

```
0001008300000001 00 KEY_LEFT /etc/lirc/lircd.conf
0001008100000001 00 KEY_DOWN /etc/lirc/lircd.conf
```

LIRC is configured correctly to support your remote control.

Controlling applications using the remote control

At this point, we have configured LIRC to recognize certain button presses on our remote control. To complete our setup, we need to tell the system what should actually happen when we press a button.

This is where the configuration file `~/.lircrc` and the application `irxevent` come into play.

1. Within your opened shell, create or edit the `~/.lircrc` file:

   ```
   $ nano ~/.lircrc
   ```

2. For each button, add a configuration section similar to the following:

   ```
   begin
      prog = irxevent
      button = KEY_0
      config = Key 0 CurrentWindow
   end
   ```

   The following screenshot shows the nano editor with the configuration for the `KEY_UP` and `KEY_DOWN` buttons:

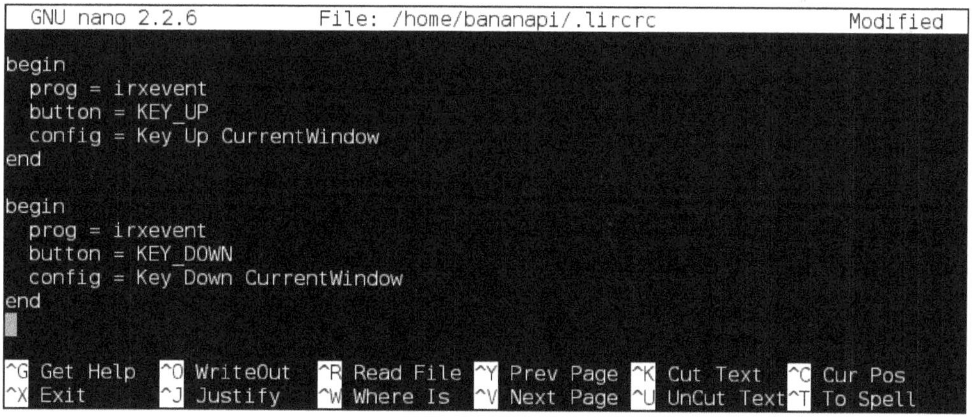

```
  GNU nano 2.2.6          File: /home/bananapi/.lircrc              Modified

begin
  prog = irxevent
  button = KEY_UP
  config = Key Up CurrentWindow
end

begin
  prog = irxevent
  button = KEY_DOWN
  config = Key Down CurrentWindow
end



^G Get Help   ^O WriteOut   ^R Read File  ^Y Prev Page  ^K Cut Text   ^C Cur Pos
^X Exit       ^J Justify    ^W Where Is   ^V Next Page  ^U UnCut Text ^T To Spell
```

3. When you have finished the configuration of each button, exit and save nano by pressing *Ctrl + X*, followed by *Y* and *Enter*.

4. Switch to your desktop if necessary, open a terminal application, and test the configuration by running the following command:

   ```
   $ irxevent
   ```

5. Push some buttons on your remote control and you should see the inputted keys on the terminal.

6. Quit the irxevent test by pressing *Ctrl + C* on your keyboard.

7. To run irxevent when the desktop is started, edit the ~/.config/lxsession/LXDE/autostart file again with nano:

   ```
   $ nano ~/.config/lxsession/LXDE/autostart
   ```

8. Add the following line:

   ```
   @irxevent -d ~/.lircrc
   ```

   The following screenshot shows the nano editor with the two applications that are autostarted:

9. Once the addition to the `autostart` file is done, exit and save nano by pressing *Ctrl + X*, followed by *Y* and *Enter*.

Your remote control is now configured completely. You will now be able to control your entire desktop using LIRC.

How it works...

In this recipe, we configured the entire LIRC setup for our remote control. LIRC is an application for decoding infrared signals sent by a remote control.

Banana Pi recognizes the infrared signals using a virtual keyboard per default. Since we want maximum flexibility by using LIRC, we need to disable that virtual keyboard. This is done via the xinput application. To permanently disable the virtual `sunxi-ir` keyboard, we execute `xinput disable sunxi-ir` every time the desktop is started by configuring the ~/.config/lxsession/LXDE/autostart file.

Then we determine the correct device file for the infrared sensor on Banana Pi. All currently available input devices are listed in the /proc/bus/input/devices process information file. As we only need to find the correct device file, we pipe the output of the input devices information to the `grep` command to filter the required line.

When we determine the correct device file (that is usually /dev/input/event0), we test the reception of infrared signals by using the evtest application. If evtest recognizes infrared signals, we know that our remote control is supported and we are ready to configure LIRC itself.

The first step is to configure which driver and device LIRC should use. This is done in the /etc/lirc/hardware.conf file. The second step is to provide a configuration for the remote control itself. Each button press on your remote control is sent as a binary code via an infrared signal. To tell LIRC which button press should be recognized as a specific key, we need to map each button code to a key. The mapping is done via the irrecord command, which requires a generic base configuration that we copied from /usr/share/lirc/remotes/generic/NEC. The irrecord program will enrich the generic configuration with the mapped keys and save the file as our actual remote control configuration (the /etc/lirc/lircd.conf file). Within the lircd.conf file, the binary codes from the remote control are converted into hex codes. Sometimes, the irrecord tool also writes button release codes to the lircd.conf which is unnecessary for our use case. Therefore, we remove the second hex codes if they were added.

When the LIRC service is restarted, the button presses on the remote control are recognized by LIRC. We test the correct input of the button presses by using the irw tool.

As a last step, we need to tell LIRC what should happen when we press a button. There are a lot of possibilities that we cannot discuss entirely. However, we use the irxevent application to control the whole desktop via our remote control. The irxevent application sends key presses to the Xorg server, just like a real keyboard. This way, we can use our remote control universally with all applications on the desktop. The key press is always sent to the graphical application that currently holds the focus.

Each button definition begins with begin and ends with end. Within each section, we define the irxevent command as the program to use via prog. The button of the remote control is mapped via button and equals to the key name in the /etc/lirc/lircd.conf. The config line defines the key press that irxevent will send to the desktop.

There's more...

Depending on your distribution, you may need to load a kernel module before you can use the infrared sensor on Banana Pi. If you do not see the sunxi-ir input device when executing cat /proc/bus/input/devices, we can try to load a kernel module:

```
$ sudo modprobe sun4i_ir
```

Or, if you use a newer kernel:

```
$ sudo modprobe sunxi_ir
```

If the input device is then recognized, you may persist the loading of the kernel module in your `/etc/modules`:

```
$ sudo -s
# echo sun4i_ir >> /etc/modules
# exit
```

We discussed the use of `irxevent` in this recipe. The default application that is shipped with the standard LIRC package is `irexec`. Using `irexec`, you can execute arbitrary commands when buttons on the remote control are pressed. Please see the official LIRC website for further information.

See also

▸ The official website of the Linux Infrared Remote Control application at `http://www.lirc.org/`

Index

A

accelerated video playback
hardware-accelerating components,
 activating 149-152
hardware-accelerating components,
 building 149-152
MPlayer, configuring 152-155
MPlayer, installing 152-155
obtaining 147, 148
references, URL 160
required components 148
VLC media player, configuring 155-160
VLC media player, installing 155-160
**Advanced Linux Sound Architecture
 (ALSA) 144**
Advanced Packaging Tool (Apt)
about 4, 33
URL 37
Android 3, 4
Apt Pinning 159
Arch Linux
URL 33
audio device
analog audio, configuring 143, 144
audio output, testing 144-146
configuring 142
HDMI pass-through, configuring 142, 143
references, URL 147

B

Banana Pi
about 1
Android, shutting down 16
booting up 15, 16

hardware components and interfaces 2, 3
hostname, determining 20
IP address, determining 20
Linux, shutting down 16, 17
operating systems 3
overview 2
pin layout 124, 125
shutting down 15, 16
URL 7
VNC server, installing 104
Banana Pro
ap6210 module, loading 42, 43
pin layout 125
reference link 127
wireless network, configuring 41, 42
wireless network, configuring with
 WiFi Config 43, 44
wireless network, manual configuration 45-47
wireless network, working 47, 48
Bash Shell Scripting
reference link 104
Bourne again shell (Bash) 22

C

Certificate Authority (CA) 90
command-line interface (CLI) 22
Cron scheduler
reference link 104

D

Database Management System (DBMS) 84
dd command 13
desktop
controlling remotely, VNC used 104-108

Digital Living Network Alliance (DLNA)
about 117
Dynamic DNS (DDNS)
about 92
hostname, updating 94, 95
setting up 93

E

external disk
booting from 59
drive, formatting 60-62
working 63

F

fdisk
URL 63
file sharing
over network, via Samba 65-74
file synchronization
Dynamic DNS (DDNS) hostname,
updating 94, 95
Dynamic DNS (DDNS), setting up 93
over Internet 92, 100-103
ownCloud, installing 96-100
port forwarding, setting up 95, 96
filesystem permissions
URL 54
fstab
configuration, URL 59
mounting via 56-58
used, for accessing Samba share on Linux 71

G

**General-Purpose input/output
pins (GPIO pins) 119**
gpio command
used, for lighting up LED 120-124
GPIO extension board
using 126
GPIO input
C code 139, 140
circuit, preparing 134
Python code 140
software, programming 136-138

using, with pushbutton 134-139
graphical user interface (GUI) 3
groups command 32

H

hard disk drives (HDD)
mounting, via SATA 54-56
hostname
determining 20-22
HTTP over SSL (HTTPS)
about 87
reference link 92

I

infrared remote control
setting up, with LIRC 166, 167
URL 174
used, for controlling applications 171-174
working 172, 173
Internet
file, synchronizing 92-103
IP address
determining 20-22

K

kernel 47
Kodi
about 160
setting up 161-166
URLs 166

L

LED
C code 132
lighting up, gpio command used 120-124
programming 127-131
programming, with C 128, 129
programming, with Python 130, 131
Python code 133
LEMP stack
setting up 86
Linux
about 4
Samba share, accessing 70

Samba share, accessing on Linux
    with fstab 71
SD card, setting up on 12-14
self-signed certificate, importing 91
SSH keys, using 112
SSH tunnel, using for VNC 108
VNC client, installing 106, 107
Linux-based operating systems
  Bananian 4
  Lubuntu 4
  Raspbian 4
LIRC
  configuring, for setting up remote
    control 167-171
  used, for setting up infrared remote
    control 166, 167

M

modprobe (probe module) command 47
MPlayer
  configuring 152-155
  installing 152-154
multimedia
  about 141
  accelerated video playback, obtaining 147
  audio device, configuring 142
  infrared remote control, setting up
    with LIRC 166
  Kodi, setting up 160
MySQL
  reference link 87
  database server, installing 78, 79

N

Nginx
  configuring 89
  URL 87
Nginx web server
  installing 75-77
  securing, SSL certificate used 87-90

O

operating systems, Banana Pi
  about 3-5

Android 3
component requisites 6
downloading 5-7
image download, URL 7
Linux 4
references 7
updating 37-41
ownCloud
  about 92
  client, configuring 103
  installing 96-100
  URL 96, 103, 104

P

PHP
  URL 87
PHP FastCGI Process Manager (PHP-FPM) 84
PhpMyAdmin
  setting up 85
PHP scripting language
  installing 77
port forwarding
  setting up 95, 96
  URL 95
pull-up/pull-down resistors
  reference link 140
pushbutton
  GPIO input, using 134-139
PuTTY
  SSH keys, using 110, 111
  SSH tunnel, adding for VNC 108
  URL 26
  used, for connecting via SSH on
    Windows 22-26
Python
  LED, programming 130, 131

R

ReadyMedia-transcode
  URL 118
rm -rf command 32
rsync
  URL 63

S

Samba
reference link 74
server, installing 66-68
shared directory, accessing on Linux
    with fstab 70-71
shared directory, accessing on
    Windows 68, 69
used, for sharing files 65-74
SD card, on Linux
setting up 12-14
SD card, on Windows
Android image, writing to 10
Linux distribution image, writing to 11
reference URLs 12
setting up 8, 9
working 11
self-signed certificate
importing, on Linux 91
importing, on Windows 90
software
installing 33, 34
packages, installing 34, 35
packages, removing 35, 36
packages, searching 34
prerequisites 33
removing 33, 34
searching 33, 34
solid state disks (SSD)
mounting, via SATA 54-56
Sound eXchange (SoX) 144
SSH
used, for connecting Banana Pi on
    Unix-like systems 27-29
used, for connecting Banana Pi with
    PuTTY 22-26
SSH keys
reference link 115
SSH password login, disabling 113, 114
used, for securing SSH 109-114
using, in PuTTY 110, 111
using, on Linux 112
SSH tunnel
adding for VNC, in PuTTY 108
reference link 109
using for VNC, on Linux 108

SSL certificate
creating 87, 88
Nginx, configuring 89
used, for securing Nginx web server 87-90
sudo command
URL 17

U

Unix-like systems
Banana Pi, connecting with SSH 27-29
UPnP media server
setting up 115-118
USB drive
mounting 49-52
working 52, 53
user
adding 30
creating 30
deleting 30-32
maintaining 29-32
password, setting 31
userdel command 32

V

**Video Decode and Presentation API for
    Unix (VDPAU) 141**
virtual hosts 102
Virtual Network Computing (VNC)
about 104
client, installing on Banana Pi 104
client, installing on Linux 106
client, installing on Windows 105, 106
reference link 109
SSH tunnel, adding in PuTTY 108
SSH tunnel, using on Linux 108
used, for controlling remote desktop 104-108
VLC media player
configuring 155-157
installing 155-158

W

web application
MySQL database server, installing 78, 79
Nginx web server, installing 75-77
PHP scripting language, installing 77

setting up 75-84
WordPress, installing 79-82
WiFi Config
used, for configuring wireless network 43, 44
Windows
Samba share directory, accessing 68, 69
SD card, setting up on 8, 9
self-signed certificate, importing 90
VNC client, installing 105, 106
wireless network
configuring, on Banana Pro 41, 42
configuring, with WiFi Config 43, 44
manual configuration 45-47
WordPress
installing 79-82

X
x11vnc VNC server
URL 109
XBMC 160

Thank you for buying
Banana Pi Cookbook

About Packt Publishing

Packt, pronounced 'packed', published its first book, *Mastering phpMyAdmin for Effective MySQL Management*, in April 2004, and subsequently continued to specialize in publishing highly focused books on specific technologies and solutions.

Our books and publications share the experiences of your fellow IT professionals in adapting and customizing today's systems, applications, and frameworks. Our solution-based books give you the knowledge and power to customize the software and technologies you're using to get the job done. Packt books are more specific and less general than the IT books you have seen in the past. Our unique business model allows us to bring you more focused information, giving you more of what you need to know, and less of what you don't.

Packt is a modern yet unique publishing company that focuses on producing quality, cutting-edge books for communities of developers, administrators, and newbies alike. For more information, please visit our website at www.packtpub.com.

About Packt Open Source

In 2010, Packt launched two new brands, Packt Open Source and Packt Enterprise, in order to continue its focus on specialization. This book is part of the Packt open source brand, home to books published on software built around open source licenses, and offering information to anybody from advanced developers to budding web designers. The Open Source brand also runs Packt's open source Royalty Scheme, by which Packt gives a royalty to each open source project about whose software a book is sold.

Writing for Packt

We welcome all inquiries from people who are interested in authoring. Book proposals should be sent to author@packtpub.com. If your book idea is still at an early stage and you would like to discuss it first before writing a formal book proposal, then please contact us; one of our commissioning editors will get in touch with you.

We're not just looking for published authors; if you have strong technical skills but no writing experience, our experienced editors can help you develop a writing career, or simply get some additional reward for your expertise.

Raspberry Pi for Secret Agents

Second Edition

ISBN: 978-1-78439-790-6   Paperback: 206 pages

Turn your Raspberry Pi into your very own secret agent toolbox with this set of exciting projects

1. Turn your Raspberry Pi into a multipurpose secret agent gadget for audio/video surveillance, Wi-Fi exploration, or playing pranks on your friends.

2. Detect an intruder on camera and set off an alarm and also find out what the other computers on your network are up to.

3. Full of fun, practical examples and easy-to-follow recipes, guaranteeing maximum mischief for all skill levels.

Learning Raspberry Pi

ISBN: 978-1-78398-282-0   Paperback: 258 pages

Unlock your creative programming potential by creating web technologies, image processing, electronics- and robotics-based projects using the Raspberry Pi

1. Learn how to create games, web, and desktop applications using the best features of the Raspberry Pi.

2. Discover the powerful development tools that allow you to cross-compile your software and build your own Linux distribution for maximum performance.

3. Step-by-step tutorials show you how to quickly develop real-world applications using the Raspberry Pi.

Please check **www.PacktPub.com** for information on our titles

Raspberry Pi Robotic Projects

ISBN: 978-1-84969-432-2   Paperback: 278 pages

Create amazing robotic projects on a shoestring budget

1. Make your projects talk and understand speech with Raspberry Pi.

2. Use standard webcam to make your projects see and enhance vision capabilities.

3. Full of simple, easy-to-understand instructions to bring your Raspberry Pi online for developing robotics projects.

Raspberry Pi Cookbook for Python Programmers

ISBN: 978-1-84969-662-3   Paperback: 402 pages

Over 50 easy-to-comprehend tailor-made recipes to get the most out of the Raspberry Pi and unleash its huge potential using Python

1. Install your first operating system, share files over the network, and run programs remotely.

2. Unleash the hidden potential of the Raspberry Pi's powerful Video Core IV graphics processor with your own hardware accelerated 3D graphics.

3. Discover how to create your own electronic circuits to interact with the Raspberry Pi.

Please check **www.PacktPub.com** for information on our titles

9 781783 552443